Written by **Certified Persuasion Specialists**

HOW TO HEAR

YES

MORE
OFTEN

Written by **Certified Persuasion Specialists**

HOW TO HEAR

YES

MORE
OFTEN

Harnessing the Power of Influence and Ethical Persuasion in Business

Patrick van der Burght - Leopold Ajami
John Doorbar - James Rose - Martin John
Mark Brown - Pilar Bringas - Isto Felin

Copyright

How to Hear YES More Often: Harnessing the Power of Influence and Ethical Persuasion in Business

1st Edition. 2024 v3.3
ASIN: B0D93RRJQL (Amazon Kindle)
ISBN: 978-1-923223-21-9 (eBook)
ISBN: 978-1-923223-22-6 (Amazon Paperback)
ISBN: 978-1-923223-23-3 (Amazon Hardcover)
ISBN: 978-1-923223-24-0 (Ingram Spark) PAPERBACK
ISBN: 978-1-923223-25-7 (Ingram Spark) HARDCOVER
ISBN: 978-1-923223-21-9 (Smashwords)

Contract the Authors:
Reach out to the authors via www.yesmoreoften.com

TRADEMARKS

Contents

About the Authors

Patrick van der Burght
Cialdini Certified Coach in Ethical Persuasion, Speaker, Entrepreneur

Leopold Ajami
Cialdini Certified Coach in Ethical Persuasion, Speaker, Trainer, and Certified Public Speaking and Thought Leadership Coach.

John Doorbar
Cialdini Certified Coach in Ethical Persuasion

James Rose
Cialdini Certified Coach in Ethical Persuasion – Trainer, Speaker and Business Coach

Martin John
Cialdini Certified Coach in Ethical Persuasion, Procurement Expert, Trainer, Coach

Mark Brown
Cialdini Certified Coach in Ethical Persuasion, Behavioural Science Expert, Coach and CEO

Pilar Bringas
Cialdini Certified Coach in Ethical Persuasion

Isto Felin
Cialdini Certified Coach in Ethical Persuasion, Strategic Renewal Consultant

Introduction

Like you, we wanted to gain insights and experience in applying the principles of influence as well as to excel in our communication and influencing skills and to do this without compromising our integrity. All the authors in this book are excited to help you better understand how to look for and ethically implement the principles of persuasion in a wide range of situations.

The original principles were set out by Dr. Robert Cialdini in his book *INFLUENCE: The Psychology of Persuasion*, which are:

Reciprocity

People tend to feel obliged to return the behaviour they receive.

Liking

People are more likely to be persuaded by those they like.

Unity

People are more influenced by those who share a common identity or group.

Social Proof

People look to others' actions to guide some of their choices.

Authority

People tend to follow the lead of credible, knowledgeable experts.

Consistency

People want to act consistently with their commitments and values.

Scarcity

People value things more when they are less available.

The principles of persuasion are universal, not industry or situation-specific. This is because we're dealing with human behaviour. Once you can see how someone successfully used a principle in one context, you will be able to 'transfer' it and put it to work in your own situation. Keep that in mind as you look through the following chapters. It is not about the particular context. It is about identifying how the principles work and recognising how to confidently activate them in your own influence challenges.

Let us give you an overview of what to expect in each chapter.

In chapter one, **Patrick van der Burght** starts us on a journey, reflecting on one of his first complete persuasion analyses of what seemed to be a dire situation when he took on the representation of a brand that had severely damaged its reputation the year before. He went from being laughed at by retailers at mentioning the brand name, to being market leader in 18 months. How did he analyse the situation and put the principles to work?

In chapter two, **Leopold Ajami** introduces the 'P.W.R.' Piece of Influence. This unique framework integrates Public Speaking, Thought Leadership, and Ethical Persuasion. It will help you develop a 'Powerline' for message precision and authority, a 'Worldview' for unique indispensability, and 'Reflection' to find your treasure in the trivial. This powerful framework is the missing piece you need to turn your voice into your most influential tool.

In chapter three, **John Doorbar** reveals how you can use the 7 principles of influence to dramatically boost your results when you present. You will follow three international managers as each of them integrates one of the factors to improve their impact. You will learn 12 practical secrets to inspire change. Some people use influence to manipulate, and you will see how to recognise these unscrupulous 'wolves'. You will then be able to easily handle any 'wolves' in sheep's clothing.

In chapter four, **James Rose** talks you through a series of examples of how different words can significantly impact your success and help you hear 'yes' more often. With the right words, you can shape people's perceptions, alter their emotions and (ethically) influence their decision-making in your favour. Once you've read this chapter, you'll never enter into a business conversation the same way again!

In chapter five, **Martin John** brings to life the impact that using the principles of ethical persuasion had in his world of Procurement and Purchasing. In four practical and relatable examples that anyone can use, read how, despite challenging circumstances, his results were transformed thanks to pre-suasion and the principles of liking, reciprocity, consistency and social proof. You'll discover that persuasion isn't just for Salespeople. Buyers will benefit from knowing these techniques, too.

In chapter six, **Mark Brown** delves into the labyrinth of decision-making within organisations. Drawn from Mark's personal experiences in a banking environment, he unveils the hidden challenges of altering established practices and overcoming resistance. It shines a light on the often-overlooked influences of cognitive biases and subconscious drivers on our decisions. This is a guide to navigating these complexities and improving decision-making processes. A must-read for those seeking to tackle the intricacies of organisational decision-making.

In chapter seven, following the example of Alexander the Great, the greatest leader of Ancient History, and his relationship with Aristotle, the towering philosopher of ancient Greece, **Pilar Bringas** explains the application of the science of human behaviour. Understanding and applying behavioural science has become the key instrument for business success, the best tool to navigate these times of fragility, anxiety and uncertainty.

In chapter eight, **Isto Felin** helps you discover the TIMBR effect – **T**iny **I**nfluence for **M**ighty **B**usiness **R**esults – a powerful approach to ethical persuasion in business. Through engaging stories and real-world examples, you'll learn how subtle applications of influence principles can drive remarkable outcomes and growth. You will also learn to connect persuasion principles to your motivations on what you want to achieve. With the help of the TIMBR effect, you can compose your own business success story.

As a suggestion, you could highlight or mark the insights that inspired you with sticky notes, and then use them as a reference guide as you revisit the book.

You will find this book an inspiration for exploring and implementing the principles of influence and persuasion. When you are ready to take the next step in developing and mastering your persuasion skills, feel free to contact any of the authors who are all certified persuasion coaches and speakers.

Enjoy your journey towards hearing YES more often.

Patrick van der Burght
Cialdini Certified Coach in Ethical Persuasion,
Speaker, Entrepreneur

ABOUT THE AUTHOR:
PATRICK VAN DER BURGHT

Patrick van der Burght is not Dr Cialdini himself but has been teaching Dr Cialdini's Principles of Persuasion to individuals and teams for over 20 years and is an active, capable and licenced **Cialdini Certified Coach**.

Patrick has a business and sales background in various industries, including real estate, aviation, high-end retail, wholesale and health. He enjoys training sales teams to master and apply Ethical Persuasion theories and helping them realise the successes that were always theirs to have by engaging the science of human decision-making and Influence.

Patrick, who is based in Australia, developed a passion and unwavering conviction for the ethical approach to persuasion in 2000 after he discovered the science explained by Dr. Cialdini. He was a sales representative at the time. He was happy with his role but frustrated by the lack of growth and success relative to his efforts.

Patrick's understanding and implementation of persuasion theory were guided by a coach who was training him to be a business consultant. Using the principles, he quickly achieved significant success. From then on, using and teaching sales professionals about persuasion became a passion.

As a valued **Cialdini Certified Coach**, he enjoys speaking and teaching on Ethical Persuasion and seeing his students progress from understanding to mastering Influence.

One of Patrick's projects is to educate young adults about persuasion as an important life skill so they can benefit from it their entire lives, be better leaders and make the world a better place.

In his free time, Patrick enjoys riding his Harley, Scuba Diving and flying small aircraft. He is happily married and loves spending time with his daughter.

Patrick van der Burght services the Australasian region and beyond. He is available for consultations, speaking, training, workshops and coaching.

Through Patrick's other business, he is also an internationally featured and published authority on creating healthier homes and has assisted ordinary families, corporate high-flyers and royalty in this field.

Further Information
The site **www.completeinfluence.com** has more information and tools. Feel free to book a 20-minute strategy call to determine your best way forward.

CHAPTER 1

Frustrated Sales Pro Turns into Scientifically-Charged Competitor

On behalf of all the authors in this book, I'd like to welcome you and compliment you on your interest in becoming more ethically persuasive. Your interest makes us all part of a select group of people willing to learn to realise the successes that were always ours to achieve without compromising our integrity.

Every chapter will provide you with different insights, all based on the same science-backed approach of Influence to help you become more capable and confident in applying your influence knowledge and hear 'YES' more often.

It's my honour to start you on this journey, so let me share an Influence experience with you to help you identify principles of persuasion to use in your situations.

How selling and competing became a lot more fun

Back in 2000, I was frustrated with my level of success in sales. I loved the industry I was in and enjoyed my role as a sales professional.

However, despite all my serious, genuine, and, I would say, 'caring' efforts towards my clients, I was not experiencing growth proportional to my efforts. The time and resources I invested produced a comfortable lifestyle, but they should have brought more success and reward for my investments.

I wanted to sell better but didn't want to lie, cheat, or deceive. Luckily, I would come across something that would improve my success rate, increase my income and reduce the money I was wasting and the stress I felt. My job, my life and competing got a lot more fun.

In this chapter, I will tell you what happened to this frustrated sales professional and share a detailed analysis of my first success story using Doctor Cialdini's Principles. The example I share is likely not from your industry, but you will be able to translate the thought process to your field or situation.

Predictably Ineffective

Now that I know better, it pains me to see sales professionals and business owners waste their time and resources on predictably ineffective communications and sales pitches in their business. Successes wouldn't be slipping through their fingers if they just knew more about the science of persuasion; it is a crying shame.

If we set out to build an aircraft, practice medicine, or work in psychology, we would only expect a great outcome if we understood the science. Yet, in sales and business (or persuasion efforts in general), most people go along daily, largely oblivious to the science available to them. The other possibility is that they know about the principles of persuasion but do not have the application skills and confidence to use them consistently and successfully. I refer to those people as the 'strugglers of influence'. Regardless of why persuasion is not used, it costs people in many ways.

Moving on from being a Struggler of Influence

While I now often work with sales professionals in high-ticket industries, I got my first lessons in persuasion elsewhere. It seems like a long time ago, but I was a sales representative in a great industry that I loved— Scuba diving wholesale.

I have had a passion for scuba diving since I was 15. I worked in scuba retail sales in the Netherlands, and thinking back now, I was already fascinated by what you could do to interact more successfully with people. My boss shared 'tactics' with me.

He knew that if we displayed the discounted watches nicely and neatly at a public event, we wouldn't sell as many as if we just 'threw' them in the display cabinet all messy.

It was magic to me. There were no sales for hours, and then they flew from our stall when we made the display look messy! While he knew this sort of thing worked, he didn't understand how.

I went to Asia to work as a dive instructor with chiselled abs and long, sun-bleached blond hair, both long gone now. Australia followed, where I stayed and eventually started my career as a sales representative for a wholesaler of scuba diving equipment. I could make money from a passion and deal with people who shared my passion, but our brand wasn't the market leader despite being a good quality brand. While I gained success, the growth was small. I felt frustrated not being able to realise more sales despite going to such great efforts. This is a frustration I recognise in so many sales professionals.

Are you tired of making all those attractive proposals and not landing them? Do you think you have a good relationship, but they are just not buying?

As luck would have it, a mentor appeared in the shape of a business consultant who my boss had hired. He developed a strategy to train us sales reps into business consultants, conducting sales training with our retailers and their staff and helping them grow and, by extension, our-selves. It was then that I was exposed to Doctor Cialdini's material for the first time. With the guidance of John, the business consultant who was training us, **I could implement Doctor Cialdini's principles and receive feedback on my understanding and use of them.** It proved so powerful to realise the successes I had been missing until then and would have continued to lose without it. My passion for teaching ethical persuasion found its way to my retailers shortly after. Their sales teams loved what I taught them, and I just loved the science and ethics of it all.

No need to be pushy, manipulative, or dishonest.

Because what I proposed to clients was presented in a way that the brain could easily make a favourable decision about, provided it was in their favour to do so, I was achieving honest and bountiful success. This is why ethical persuasion benefits both parties involved and creates long-last-ing relationships. It is why I love what I do.

The success that solidified my passion for ethical persuasion

It was incredible. A good, high-ticket product with a small market share had destroyed its reputation by accident the year before, and I built it to the market leader in 18 months. From this example, you will get an insight into where and how to look for the principles in your situations. I'll take you through the principles and explain how I used them. The product is likely unrelated to what you do, but that doesn't matter for learning. Whether in real estate, medical equipment, aircraft, automotive or other high-end sales, persuasion is all about human decision-making.

This is why I wasn't a Struggler of Influence for long

In a way, I was lucky. Lucky in the sense that my introduction to the principles of influence came with the guidance of an experienced business consultant who was reasonably capable of identifying available principles in a situation and coming up with ideas on how to use them. This doesn't happen to everyone who bumps into Doctor Cialdini's teachings. Too often, someone finally becomes aware of the principles and their power, but then they don't develop the application skill to use them.

Despite how easy the principles are to understand, you cannot learn how to use persuasion properly, successfully and automatically by just reading a book, attending a presentation or workshop, watching many webinars, or reading newsletters. We need repetition to increase the retention of new information. Then, have someone skilled confirm that you are doing or interpreting things correctly or have them correct your understanding.

The product was an Australian-made dry diving suit, and I was their new Australian representative in approximately 2001. My territory contained the colder states and, therefore, prime target areas. I've used many different styles of dry diving suits recreationally and in the military, but this suit was better than all of them. It was made of 2 separate layers: An inner membrane water-tight suit (that you could fix like a bicycle tyre inner tube in 5 minutes if you had to) and an outer suit protecting the inner suit very well. The problem was that the year before, they had changed suppliers for the inner suit material, and after some months of use, **all the suits that were sold that year started to delaminate. A disaster. Every single one had to be replaced.**

You can imagine what reception I got when entering retail stores and announcing I had picked up representation for 'HotnDry'. They laughed at me and expressed no interest in selling this brand. I was then confronted with their new nickname for this company: ColdnClammy. I knew I had a problem, and my focus turned to the science of persuasion to find out what help I could find.

What is in the situation?

When someone knows the seven principles and is aware of their activators and amplifiers, **they need to use their creativity and situational awareness to identify which principles are in the situation.** Engaging them may mean bringing bits of information into the audience's awareness, changing the order in which things are presented, or sometimes changing the steps people take. Let's tally some of the facts that were in my influence challenge:

- I had this great product made locally.

- Not many divers have used a product like this before. The air in the suit and undergarments compresses and expands during depth

changes, and as the air can move around in the suit when changing your angle, people can be worried about operating it safely or
comfortably.

- Retailers often needed more staff, and staff typically needed better sales skills.

- I had extensive experience with other suits of this type, but I
was relatively young, which wouldn't automatically reflect my
experience.

- I was quite an experienced dive instructor and had been diving in
the army.

- I wanted retailers to at least stock the two models for display so
they would be committed to the suit and brand and show their
commitment to clients.

Now that I'm a Certified Influence Coach, I would have used so many more
things to my advantage, but here is what I did at the time, which was very
effective. **Think about how you could use this in your industry.**

CONTRAST – What you present first matters

- Because retailers could purchase directly from a local manufacturer, our price was lower than foreign brands that wholesal-
ers would import and put their margin on. This was easy. I could
compare the price of imported dry diving suits against ours and
highlight incredible value whilst countering the assumption that
'more expensive must be better'.

- We had two different models of suits and the option to tailor-make
them to personal measurements and add accessories. Therefore, I
could first mention the cost of a customised top-of-the-line model
with all the optional extras. Then, mention its price without cus-
tomisation and accessories, and lastly, discuss the base model,
which had no available add-on options.

RECIPROCITY - How can you genuinely help your audience?

- I presented retailers with the offer to host drysuit trials. I would bring 10-12 suits in different sizes and would offer to present about drysuit diving and its advantages and disadvantages in their store. Then, I would take their clients to a nearby pool to try the suits. If we made any sales, the retailer would put the order in as usual and make their normal profit.

- The trial would give them a free event to promote and look proactive with, an extra person to conduct this with (me), and significant income without significant outlay if we made sales. The trial was quite a valuable opportunity for the retailer.

- The divers (clients) were not charged for the presentation, pool entry, or equipment use, regardless of whether they wanted to buy a suit.

LIKING - You can be a good friend

- My retailers knew me reasonably well, and we clearly had similar interests and often backgrounds as instructors. However, they learned a lot more about me (our similarities) when I asked them to introduce me and gave them a list of my credentials to use (authority).

- During my presentation, I would ask clients to share their stories and experiences, let them know if there were any similarities between us, and give compliments if they were genuinely possible.

- When answering questions in the shop and when trying the suits in the pool, I would compliment people on their understanding and/or use of the suits.

- I made a big effort to impart as much knowledge as possible to give people a valuable learning experience. This also worked towards their goal of learning something from the experience regardless of whether they made a purchase. I was, therefore, working towards a common goal.

- Similarly, the retailer needed to make a profit. While I stood to benefit, I went above and beyond the call of duty to work towards a profitable event for the retailer.

UNITY - What community do you both feel part of?

- This principle had not been identified at this time, but I acted on it from a similarity perspective, as we have in Liking.

- For the retailers, I was an instructor like them, and I made sure they knew.

- For the clients, I was a diver like them.

- If the event was in Melbourne, I was a Melbournian like them.

- If it was interstate and I noticed one of the divers had a Dutch last name, I'd point out we had the same heritage.

AUTHORITY - Trustworthy expertise?

- As soon as I was confronted with the negative attitude from retailers towards the brand, I started using that as a weakness that I could volunteer. "HotnDry made a major blunder last year, and despite people having had their suits updated, it was a big inconvenience to everyone involved, but... HotnDry are back with the original manufacturer of the inner membrane material, and they have learned a valuable lesson. The suits are now better than ever before." Most retailers were then open to discussing and investigating possibilities.

- Before the presentation portion of the trial started, I insisted that a store person give me a formal introduction, for which I gave them a list of my credentials, experience and achievements.

- As I was relatively young (about 28), I asked the store person to start the introduction with "I know he looks rather young, but..." before they mentioned my credentials. This would, as you know, make the whole introduction more believable.

- The introduction included my certification as an instructor and mentioned my military drysuit diving experience, raising their perception of me as an authority.

- Personal photos were used in the presentation, showing me using drysuits recreationally and in the army.

- Photos of commercial divers (underwater construction) in the suit were also shown, building the authority and confirming the suits were durable.

SOCIAL PROOF - Which positive actions of others could you share?

- As soon as retailers started to accept the offer to host trials, this was used as social proof. When proposing to schedule an event, I made sure to let retailers know how many other retailers like them had already planned trials with me.

- During the presentation, I would remind attendees (who typically dived in wetsuits) about the increasing amount of drysuit divers they would have seen on diving sites. Hereby showing they were getting more popular. In a joke, I would also remind them how much more comfortable and generally 'not freezing' drysuits divers are when they exit the water and how they are always the last to come out. This reminded them of the social proof that people use these suits and that it allowed those divers to enjoy themselves more.

- Before the event, I would ask the retailer if they knew anyone likely to order a suit. I also focused on judging the enthusiasm of the attendees. At the event's conclusion, I would then ask the most likely-to-buy person if they wanted to order a suit, hoping to get a prompt or enthusiastic 'yes'. This then encouraged others to order.

- When ordering a suit and choosing the optional extras, I was sure to point out which were the most popular accessories, which made them even more popular.

SCARCITY – We value more what is rare or scarce

- When I proposed hosting a trial to retailers, there was natural scarcity in the available evenings and weekends on which this could be done. The onset of the winter season would also motivate clients to buy a suit to use during a full winter instead of half the winter.

- When it came to promoting the event, there was natural scarcity. I only had 10-12 suits to bring, and because we needed different sizes, we had to limit the trial to a maximum of 8 people.

- In the presentation, comparing their experiences in a wetsuit and getting cold as the dive progressed, it was ethical to point out that drysuit divers dive longer and enjoy the first minute as much as the last. Without a drysuit, anyone would lose that enjoyment. Considering the investment of time and money to get to a dive site, a drysuit would stop you from wasting money on shorter, more uncomfortable dives.

- Of course, the suit's unique features received enough attention. When it came to choosing accessories, I was sure to point out what benefits and enjoyment would not be received if they were not included and that it was a lot cheaper to add them when ordering a new suit instead of adding them later.

- Most people would buy the top-of-the-line and pick their own colours and accessories. To get the suit made for them would take a couple of weeks. Delaying the placement of an order would mean the suit would arrive later, with less winter to enjoy. Other orders being placed first could also make the production time longer and delay receiving it—all reasons to order now.

- We didn't offer a hefty discount on the day, but we did offer a free pocket accessory for the top-of-the-line suit if ordered on the day.

CONSISTENCY - Small to bigger public steps

- Retailers were asked to communicate the planned trial to the client base as soon as we set the date and displayed a notice in the shop. This would reduce any chances of them cancelling.

- Divers were asked to write their names on the publicly displayed sign-in sheet, which showed other divers that available spots were reducing (scarcity). As their writing was public, active and voluntary, cancellations and no-shows were very few.

- During the presentation portion, people were asked if they would enjoy their dives more if they had certain benefits available to them. A positive answer would be a small verbal and public statement. Then, when the trial itself was positive, and they expressed that they liked or loved it, that was another statement. Of course, not everyone would buy a suit on the night, but our conversion rate was high.

If I had been properly trained in persuasion, I could have done more and heard yes even more often, but I achieved impressive results by doing what I did back then. I trust this analysis of my influence steps helps you to look for and use the principles in your influence challenges.

Stop being a Struggler of Influence

In this chapter, I shared how this frustrated sales professional found the powerful skills that made all the difference without resorting to manipulation, lying, or cheating. You read a detailed analysis of my first big success story using Doctor Cialdini's Principles, and I trust you got inspiration from it. You can now translate the thought process to your field or situation and reclaim more of the successes you're currently losing.

The skilled application of Persuasion has a big impact on results.

Salespeople will not be well-equipped without properly formed application skills and will not consistently identify and successfully use or benefit from the principles.

Your path forward

It is time for you to fully develop the application skills of Ethical Persuasion and apply this crucial science to your everyday communications. Stop wasting time and resources, and move to your objectives more quickly. With confidence in the scientific validity of your persuasive efforts, you will have more fun competing and enjoy the things, experiences, and people you hold dear.

When you or your team have had enough of trying to do without, I would be delighted to assist you with formal training or consulting.

Free tools for learning

If you like, you can access some valuable free tools on my website here:

www.completeinfluence.com/readers/

From a no-strings downloadable guide to my FREE 90-minute video introductory courses on ethical persuasion, tailored to various industries or situations, and other helpful tools. It is not as comprehensive as if you or your team went through training and coaching with me (which can include certification and a lifetime accreditation!), and it would lack the development of confidence and application skill, but it will introduce or refresh your understanding of the principles very well and give you practical examples.

If you found this chapter valuable, please leave an honest review on the website of your favourite online retailer.

I wish you an influential future!

Leopold Ajami
Cialdini Certified Coach in Ethical Persuasion, Speaker, Trainer, and
Certified Public Speaking and Thought Leadership Coach

ABOUT THE AUTHOR: LEOPOLD AJAMI

You've climbed to the top, but does your voice echo your achievements?

In a world where everyone's shouting, how do you ensure your voice doesn't just echo but leaves a mark?

Leopold Ajami is the designer behind leaders' most powerful tool: their voice.

He's a Certified Public Speaking and Thought Leadership Coach, a Cialdini-Certified Coach, and a trainer in Ethical Persuasion.

Leopold's mission is to transform leaders into ethical influencers by designing a voice that amplifies their worth.

After a two-decade, multi-disciplinary career in creative advertising, strategy, design thinking, filmmaking, and even teaching practical Philosophy to innovators, this eclectic mix led Leopold to initiate the birth of the 'Ph.C System'—a unique integration of Philosophy, Creativity, and Communication tailored to transform leaders into designers of decisions.

Dr. Robert Cialdini's principles of persuasion not only improved the 'Ph.C System' but also transformed Leopold and his clients into passionate detectives of human nature and flourishing.

Leopold is a 2x founder, and in 2019, he started the Novel Philosophy Academy to empower ambitious leaders to sharpen their thinking, amplify their influence, and build their brand as distinguished thought leaders.

With a client roster featuring top executives from renowned companies like Google, Apple, Meta, Booz Allen, and Russell Reynolds, Leopold's scientific approach is tested and proven. He focuses on training, consultancy, coaching, and designing transferrable and scalable frameworks.

Imagine persuading your audience with such clarity, confidence, and creativity that they don't merely hear you but are moved by you. That's the transformative experience Leopold offers.

As an international speaker, Leopold has touched lives across the US, Europe, the Middle East, and Africa. A conference organizer dubbed him "The Netflix of The Stage" because of his innovative technique of structuring ideas and speeches into gripping stories that leave audiences yearning for more.

Yet, Leopold's ultimate goal is to help you amplify your worth by designing an influential voice.

Contact Leopold Ajami for a complimentary 30-minute discovery call. Leopold is also available for podcasts, corporate training, and speaking engagements.

Connect via LinkedIn: https://www.linkedin.com/in/leopoldajami/

CHAPTER 2

Give Them A Piece Of You

By Leopold Ajami

I took away something precious from my 4-year-old daughter.

"Daddy!" The urgency in her tiny voice as I interrupted her, mid-sentence, stopped me cold. She looked up in frustration. "Daddy! I lost my question!"

Not forgot. Lost!

Like a balloon slipping from her fingers, a piece of her curiosity had vanished into thin air.

Have you ever felt that? Your ideas, your opportunities, your voice, slipping away?

That's when it dawned on me. My daughter, in her tiny articulation, had taught me something tremendous about persuasion:

You can't influence people unless you first give them a piece of you.

Imagine standing on the edge of greatness, but somehow, you're invisible. Your meticulous presentations meet blank stares. Your groundbreaking proposals fall flat. In that moment, you're thinking, "This is it!" But instead of rewards, all you get is silence or rejection.

I've been there. We all have.

Almost everything you do depends on your power to persuade yourself to make better decisions, and on others choosing you.

How can you influence people to move in your direction? By taking a 'Piece of You', designing a bridge into their hearts and minds, and compelling them to walk your path.

And the tool for building this bridge? It's surprisingly simple: Your Voice.

Persuasion has been used unethically to manipulate, propagandize, and lead people to disastrous consequences; force and fraud have reigned over words.

However, morality is a choice; we choose to be ethical persuaders, which means standing on the side of truth, being rational, and trading value for value. Your persuasion must help others make wiser decisions and provide a bridge to guide them toward better results. Flourishing in life should be the obvious choice.

As an ethical persuader, you cannot afford to get lost in the noise. Your vision, which could reshape the world, cannot remain caged in your mind. Your voice, rich with potential, should not go unrecognized. It's unjust for you, and for anyone who could benefit from your thought leadership.

Justice demands that you design a voice that amplifies your worth.

In this chapter, you will discover the **P.W.R. Piece of Influence**, a distinctive framework that integrates the science of ethical persuasion, public speaking, and thought leadership.

You'll uncover:

- **Powerline** for message-anchoring and authority
- **Worldview** for unparalleled uniqueness and connection
- **Reflection** for finding treasure in the trivial.

By the end of the chapter, you'll have practical tools to turn your voice into your most powerful tool of influence.

Powerline

Like me, you will have used some or all of the universal principles of persuasion many times, whether by design or default. However, at a tech conference on 20 July 2018, these principles were far from my mind because I was focused on Michelle, the next speaker, and the first woman appointed CEO of a big tech company.

You know the scene: coffee in hand and a circle of people around her, she is lost in thought and steam. She was trying to remember and rehearse her upcoming speech, while remaining polite, smiling and nodding.

Giving Michelle a gentle nudge, I drew her out offering a lifeline. She later thanked me for rescuing her. A simple gesture bridges the distance between strangers.

"Why is your talk important?"

I tapped on her pre-stage nerves. She spoke with passion and purpose. She shared how her tech journey had reshaped her character and enhanced her empathy with every user touched by her innovations. Yet, despite her moving story, a crucial piece remained missing – a **Powerline** to anchor her main idea and influence her audience.

When she finished, I said, "Thank you for sharing a lesson I will never forget."

Had you been there, you'd have seen her lean in, eager for the lesson! In a whisper, like sharing a gift meant only for her, I said:

"What you build, builds you!"

You could see the tension immediately leaving her body and the smile in her eyes when she screamed, "Oh, can I borrow that line?"

I gave her a piece of me. But here's what's so fascinating: that piece was always hers; I just helped her uncover it.

What is a Powerline?

It's a concise, memorable sentence that captures the essence of your message. It's your lesson or words of wisdom crafted to stick and spark long after being spoken. Keep it short, simple, and, if possible, rhythmic (like children's books).

Ethical persuaders use a Powerline to uncover:

- **the Real:** insights grounded in facts

- **the Hidden:** not overblown but finely highlighted to elevate understanding. (Her story, framed by my words)

- **the Valuable:** notice that the Powerline goes beyond Michelle's journey; it carries a universal wisdom for her audience.

Michelle owned the stage and influenced her audience. They remembered, repeated, and resonated with her Powerline.

And who was the first person she chose to speak with after her talk? Yours truly. Not because I'm special, but because I activated the seed that gives rise to influence: "Give Them a Piece of You."

Tiny Words, Tremendous Worth.

This instant connection with Michelle, who later became my client, exemplifies Reciprocity and Authority in action—principles central to persuasion.

1. Reciprocity

Words possess an extraordinary power—they can uplift, heal, and transform. Crafted with care and intention, they become one of the most invaluable **gifts** we can offer, activating a cycle of giving and receiving that enriches both parties.

Think of the Powerline as a **gift of distilled wisdom** that prompts your audience to engage, share, and act on your message. Unlike tangible gifts, words shape your psyche — they can affirm your worth, ignite your potential, and comfort your pains.

When have you expressed what others struggle to articulate?

With the Powerline, you give them the words they need for the time they'll need them. Your audience, clients, customers, and friends need your words as their shortcut to wisdom.

However, the simplicity of the Powerline can be deceiving. To be effective in persuasion, ensure you frame it as a gift. Thank them for the lesson so they are mentally ready to hear your words. Or tease them before you tell them.

There's nothing profound about "One more thing...", as coined by Steve Jobs. However, he transformed it into a Powerline by framing it to the audience as a gift of innovation, joy, and wonder, as well as exciting speculation among the media, deepening their psychological investment in what was to come. He gave us a piece of Apple's ingenuity and commitment to pushing boundaries.

2. Authority

Authority isn't about exerting power or force; it's about guiding with your knowledge, expertise, and trustworthiness, without relying on titles. The

Powerline does that by cutting through the noise, demanding attention, and cementing your credibility — ultimately activating the principle of authority.

Our minds are pattern-seeking machines. We're wired to latch onto meaningful, concise wisdom that resonates with our values, challenges our perceptions, or illuminates a truth we've missed.

When you nail that Powerline, you're not just sharing words; you're transmitting worth.

Andrew's story is a case in point.

Dedicated to transforming the lives of youth in Zambia, Andrew, who was one of my students, became aware of a hidden truth. The lack of skills development among Zambian youth left them with a dire choice: a dead-end job or fall into a despair so deep it sometimes led to suicide! Andrew's mission was clear, but his fundraising pitch needed the nudge of influence.

"Thank you, Andrew, for sharing this important lesson with me," I said.

He leaned in. He had worked with me before, so knew a Powerline was coming.

"In Zambia, the opposite of skill is — suicide!"

Bam! One line essentialized his message and highlighted a critical, yet neglected, point of view. Typically, lack of skill leads to incompetence or inability, not to the extreme of suicide, and that was the stark contrast the youth faced. This Powerline immediately positioned Andrew as a thought leader because it did more than summarize the crisis; it threw a spotlight on a harsh reality overlooked by many — but not Andrew.

He didn't need any title; he offered his audience a thunderous wake-up call by reframing the issue in a way that demanded attention, affinity, and action.

Consider this Powerline (and feel free to borrow or Tweet it):

Most people restate problems; persuaders reframe them.

Before you read on, consider the lessons or insights you've gathered so far in this chapter or other chapters you have read. What would your Powerline be? Share it with me, and we can refine it together. (That's my promise to you.)

The P.W.R. Piece Of Influence

Activates the principles of:
Reciprocity & Authority

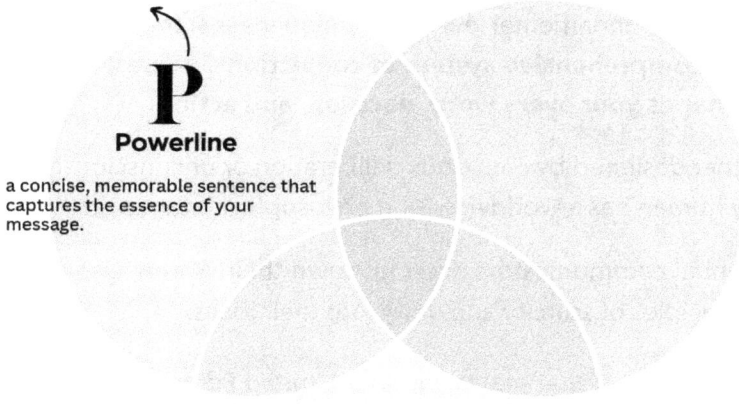

P
Powerline

a concise, memorable sentence that captures the essence of your message.

Powerline

Ask yourself:

- Can you distill your main idea into one unforgettable line?

- Does your Powerline spark curiosity, depth and emotions?

- Is it particular to your story yet universal enough to inspire your audience?

Worldview

Why does the notion of "Limited Edition" captivate us?

It's a psychological trigger signaling a uniqueness that won't last forever. That's scarcity at work. We tend to value what is scarce, be it exclusivity, time, or quantity. But there's much more to scarcity.

You!

You are an irreplaceable, unrepeatable, unique being. But is the world witnessing your true essence?

At the most fundamental level, your uniqueness stems from your Worldview: **a comprehensive system of convictions, values, and attitudes that shapes your every word, decision, and action.**

Whether designed by conscious deliberation or unconsciously acquired, every human has a Worldview — a philosophical stance on life.

Influential communicators don't just own their Worldviews, they weave the principles of scarcity and unity into their ideas.

- **Scarcity:** What marks you as a 'Limited Edition'? Scarcity isn't just found, it's formed.

- **Unity:** How does your Worldview connect and mobilize others around shared values?

I've lived many lives.

I've had my share of time in the corporate, consultancy, and entrepreneurial worlds, and my thirst for learning led me to study various subjects.

But it was philosophy that lit the fire under me.

I felt unstoppable. I could see connections where others saw chaos, crafting arguments that felt bulletproof. Charged with this newfound power,

I launched an academy where leaders could forge unshakable foundations. I was boring, preachy, and unempathetically radical — and I failed! I had no influence that sparked the same fire in them.

Then, my wife Zeina gave me a wake-up call. She told me flat out, "Your message is too complex. You speak as if you know all the answers and sound too arrogant! It's not you."

Of course, I disagreed and blamed the world for not being ready for real depth. With eyes that cut straight to the truth, Zeina then shattered my defenses. I'll never forget what she said:

"Walls don't get goosebumps!"

What was she talking about? Of course, walls can't feel! Pfffttt. But as the words sank in, I realized she was right. (She's always right.) I'd been treating people like walls and expecting them to feel and understand my ideas. But "Walls don't get goosebumps!"

Worse, I had become a wall myself, isolating my ideas from the very life they were meant to enrich. I was failing to influence because I was engaged in wall-to-wall communication.

Zeina's words helped me see my mistakes and improve my methods. She gave me a piece of her, which became my Worldview! There are many world-class speakers and coaches out there, but "walls don't get goosebumps" is now my Limited Edition Worldview on communication. It defines a problem (wall-to-wall communication), implies a novel way to solve it (empathy and shared unity), and guides the audience from passive to active engagement and toward a new understanding.

How can you refine your Worldview?

1. **Give them a piece of you**: Uniqueness doesn't require invention. It's new if it's about you.

2. **Own the problem before sharing your Worldview**: When you're seen as profoundly involved in framing a specific problem — like Uber was with the inconvenience of cab-hailing — people naturally look to you for solutions.

3. **Strive not for a 'better' worldview but a 'different' one**: Apple doesn't compete for better products; they are a rebellion against the status quo.

Your influence stems from how you see the world and how others see it through you.

Unique and United

But here's the twist: a worldview that unites can either propel us toward darkness or enlightenment.

Adolf Hitler had an unethical worldview. It united one group against another through manipulation and force, which led to the exclusion, persecution, and genocide of those who did not belong.

In the 1960s, many people dreamed of equality and justice. It took one person to frame an ethical worldview that we know and remember as "I have a dream!"

Sometimes, the contrast is not just between good and evil — but between the implicit and the explicit.

One of my clients, an Early Childhood Development entity, struggled to persuade parents of the benefits of play, not only for their children's growth and confidence, but also the parents' well-being. It seems obvious, but parenting is like running a marathon with no finish line in sight. Too often, the easiest shortcut is letting screens babysit.

My clients tried everything — ads, workshops, influencer shout-outs — nothing stuck.

Drawing from Dr. Cialdini's wisdom on the principle of unity, we understand that individuals are more likely to be influenced by those with whom they have a shared identity or connection. Parents inherently share a bond with their kids, but it often hums implicitly in the background. What if we could turn up the volume on that connection, making it something they could touch, feel, and experience?

The solution was simple: we invited parents to become children again by spending a day in the playground. Imagine adults on trampolines and swings, their faces filled with confusion, shyness, and anticipation.

Just like that, the transformation began. Skeptical faces turned into laughter; silence broke into conversation; and tiredness gave way to joy. Even as they caught their breath, they asked for ice cream, mirroring the behavior of their children. It was a profound shift — from implicit to explicit unity that brought down walls, and opened hearts and minds. Parents realized that unity wasn't just about shared blood and space, but about shared experiences, laughter, and — yes — even shared exhaustion. Now, they were more willing to collaborate with us on strategies to deepen their bond with their children.

The takeaway?

Never take a shared worldview for granted — light it up so it's explicit and tangible.

This makes me wonder: How might we shape a better world with the courage to give voice to the unspoken bonds that unite us?

As you read on, notice how the **P.W.R. Piece** weaves together, with each part unlocking the next level of influence.

The P.W.R. Piece Of Influence

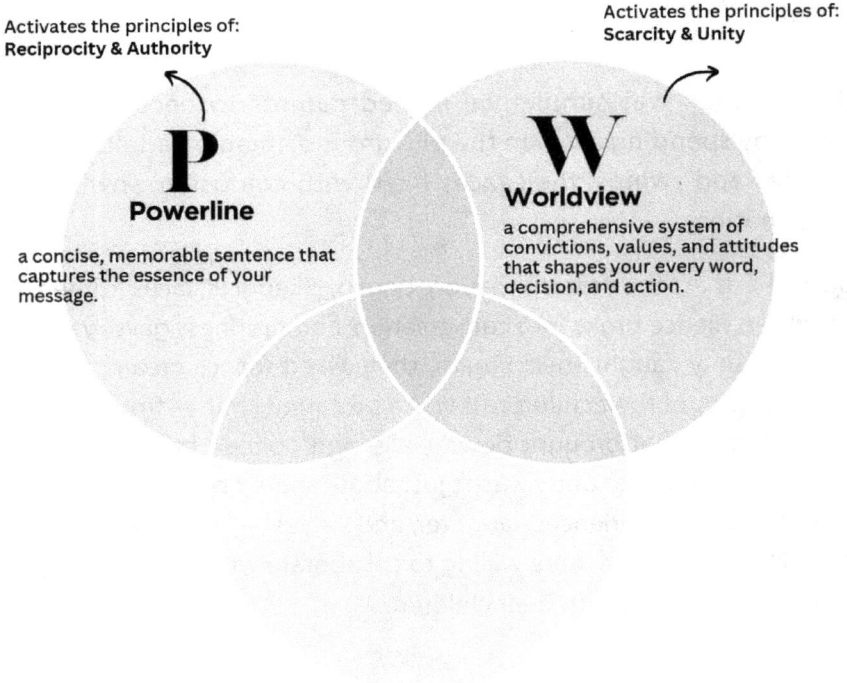

Activates the principles of:
Reciprocity & Authority

Activates the principles of:
Scarcity & Unity

P
Powerline

a concise, memorable sentence that
captures the essence of your
message.

W
Worldview

a comprehensive system of
convictions, values, and attitudes
that shapes your every word,
decision, and action.

Powerline

Ask yourself:

- Can you distill your main idea
  into one unforgettable line?

- Does your Powerline spark
  curiosity, depth and emotions?

- Is it particular to your story yet
  universal enough to inspire your
  audience?

Worldview

Ask yourself:

- What sets your view apart from the
  crowd?

- Does your worldview truly connect
  with its intended audience?

- Are you building a movement for
  your audience to unite around your
  ideas and see themselves in your
  words?

Reflection

My mom was a heavy smoker for over four decades. She then quit for ten years, holding onto life with a commitment that inspired everyone around her. Then she started having a cigarette or two. Despite the obvious risks and health complications, she couldn't see the harm. I was bewildered and determined to change her mind.

Have you ever had a challenge that mocked your entire arsenal of skills?

I used every logical argument in the book.

"Smoking's bad for you, Mom," I said.

Indifferent, she replied, "Son, I'm too old to care about what's good for me."

It was time to switch gears and start tugging at heartstrings.

"Don't you want to see your grandkids grow up?" More of a prayer than a question.

"I'm doing just that, sweetie. A cigarette or two won't matter."

How do you persuade someone who thinks they've got nothing to lose?

Worse, I had nothing to offer her.

Pay attention; it pays back and forth.

Every day, I indulge in a little reflective ritual. It's simple: observe and reflect. Then write—even if it's only one line. It could be anything: a fleeting conversation, a peculiar cloud, a child's laughter. Reflection helps me find patterns and meaning and is often the key to unlocking stubborn challenges.

Sometimes, one line turns into a social media post, a conversation starter, or a framework for my coaching.

For example, once, while playing with my daughter, I noticed there are two ways to give children candy. You can offer it and receive a thank-you, or turn the candy into an experience:

"Close your eyes. There's something for you. No peeking. Ta-da! Here's your special candy."

When you give an experience, you get an unmatchable response.

Upon reflection, I noticed the similarities between offering candy and delivering words in a presentation. This became what I now call "The Candy Principle" and is integral to my Public Speaking programs. Of course, it also led to an unexpected Powerline:

Make your words sweet or sour, but never stale.

Reflection is not optional; it's how you find your treasure in the trivial.

I didn't realize, however, that it's the silent power that supercharges persuasion! It enriches your empathetic spirit and detective-like interest in human nature and behavior. And it allows those you are persuading to reflect on their own lives!

Goodbye, Mom.

One day, a seemingly trivial photo of Mom on my phone caught my eye.

She was just waving goodbye from her balcony. Then I reflected: What's happening? Why is it important? How do I feel about it? There was depth in this photo.

All my life, Mom's behaved the same way — without fail. Every time I leave her house, she goes to her balcony, waves goodbye, and watches over me until I'm out of sight. Every. Single. Time. Through every season or mood swing, there she was, a constant sentinel.

Suddenly, it clicked.

Mom had something to lose!

Now, I had a plan. I asked Mom to prepare my favorite dish and invited friends and family. I revealed the balcony photo and shared the story. They were fascinated, but you should have seen Mom — beaming with pride and joy.

I turned to her and said, "Mom, this is an achievement. Do you still feel you must watch over me — even now, at my age?"

"Of course," she replied, heavy with decades of unspoken love and commitment.

"And, would you say it takes integrity to uphold such a commitment?"

Her eyes twinkled, "Yes, of course!"

"So, you're a person of integrity then?"

"You little…" she snapped with a smile. "You bet I am. That's all I've got!"

And there it was — a lever of persuasion hidden in plain sight. All I needed was a final, gentle nudge to remind Mom of her own integrity and commitments:

"You said you would quit smoking all those years ago, and you did! Do you still have what it takes to stay true to your words?"

She didn't just say yes, she had to say yes!

Why?

I'd activated the principle of consistency, which states that people are more likely to commit to what they have previously said and done. It wasn't about smoking anymore. It was about being true to herself, and to the legacy of her life-long commitments. Saying no would have been a breach of her integrity.

And her integrity was the one thing she could not afford to lose.

Consider the following four tactics for your influence challenge.

1. **Highlight their commitments**: Illuminate the values and actions that define your audience. Make their own words the foundation for persuasion.

2. **Collect tiny yeses**: They are the stepping stones to higher commitments.

3. **Make them commit in public**: Whether online or in a group, committing puts their words and deeds on the line, fortifying their self-image and integrity. Mom committed in front of family and friends —she'd need to find new ones to sneak a smoke from.

4. **Reflect consistently**: This is the game-changer! You will connect dots you didn't even know were there. One trivial observation can be the key to unlocking an unforeseen treasure for you and those you want to influence.

The P.W.R. Piece Of Influence

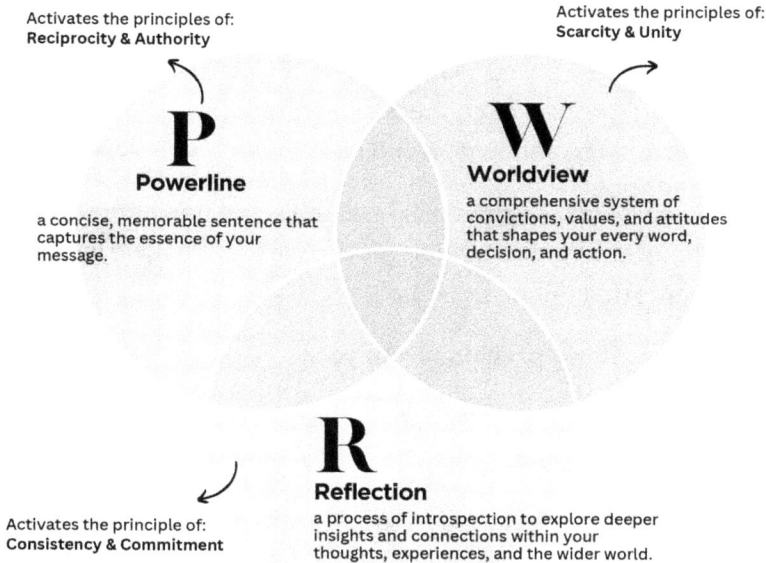

Activates the principles of:
Reciprocity & Authority

Activates the principles of:
Scarcity & Unity

P
Powerline

a concise, memorable sentence that captures the essence of your message.

W
Worldview

a comprehensive system of convictions, values, and attitudes that shapes your every word, decision, and action.

R
Reflection

a process of introspection to explore deeper insights and connections within your thoughts, experiences, and the wider world.

Activates the principle of:
Consistency & Commitment

Powerline

Ask yourself:

- Can you distill your main idea into one unforgettable line?

- Does your Powerline spark curiosity, depth and emotions?

- Is it particular to your story yet universal enough to inspire your audience?

Worldview

Ask yourself:

- What sets your view apart from the crowd?

- Does your worldview truly connect with its intended audience?

- Are you building a movement for your audience to unite around your ideas and see themselves in your words?

Reflection

Ask yourself:

- Do you reflect to find meaning even in the most mundane observations?

- How can you transform insights gained through reflection into actionable influence strategies?

- Does your thought process inspire others to reflect and grow?

What's your balcony photo?

Whenever I share this story about Mom, my audience reflects on their loved ones. They see the universal principle and are curious about how it applies to their situation.

Why?

Persuasion isn't merely an outward process directed toward others. It starts as an inward process of connection and reflection. It's about paying attention to what is, and what could be.

Words, worldviews, and principles are invaluable, but not without shared moments of reflection that remind us of who we are, what we value, and the commitments that define us.

I have taken something precious from you!

I have taken a piece of your attention, curiosity, and time. What's more, I've taken a piece of your soul.

When planning this chapter, I wanted to write about the ideas I wish I had known about as I became a designer of decisions. But I was also thinking about you and whether my thoughts, words, and stories would resonate and touch your life.

You influenced me. Now, I invite you to give the world a piece of your influence.

Take the **P.W.R. Piece of Influence** beyond the pages of this book.

Here's your first move: Reflect deeply and choose a piece of you — a defining story, a flash of insight, or a question that won't leave you alone. Distill it into a Powerline, share it, and watch the power of hearing 'YES' more often!

This tiny tweak is a tremendous leap toward designing a voice that amplifies your worth.

John Doorbar,
Cialdini Certified Coach in Ethical Persuasion

ABOUT THE AUTHOR: JOHN DOORBAR

John Doorbar is an international entrepreneur, trainer and author. He is British and focuses his attention on teaching in the unique area of Persuading with Ethical Influence.

John has written three training books. The first two are about excellent business communication skills; the third is entitled *What Happy People Know*. This book's premise is that we all have the potential to be genuinely happy no matter what is happening around us. We can learn this too.

John has taught at 18 Fortune 500 companies as well as at the European Union in Strasbourg. He has travelled in 13 countries across Europe and in the USA. He offers high-value Professional Speakers Training to executives who need to persuade audiences to change their behaviour.

His work is based on 25 years of his own research, drawing together the best state-of-the-art scientifically proven insights. This research includes the works of Dr Robert Cialdini (the best-selling author of the book, *Influence: Science and Practice*) and Dr B.J. Fogg (*Persuasive Technology and Tiny Habits*).

John's philosophy of teaching is that his clients have within them the potential to become truly great speakers regardless of whether they are introverts or extroverts. His focus is on guiding his clients through a process, taking them from where they are now to where they want to be. In this process, his clients learn to trust their implicit skills so that they can speak naturally in front of an audience of any size.

John's vision is to help entrepreneurs and business executives so that they can support people both within and outside their company. For people who ask for John's support as a coach or mentor, it's important that they fulfil some important criteria, such as being:

- **Optimistic**: you see a future that is better than the present.
- **Resourceful**: especially around time and money.
- **Personally responsible**: accountable for your actions.
- **Confident** in making decisions.
- **Enjoyable** to spend time with, and are willing to work hard and play hard.

You can find further information on his website at www.johndoorbar.com.

CHAPTER 3

Twelve Secrets to Boost Your Presenting Results

By John Doorbar

"There is nothing either good or bad but thinking makes it so."

– William Shakespeare in Hamlet

The Ethical Side of Influence

Let's start this chapter with a metaphor — the "knife metaphor".

Any powerful tool can be used for good or for evil. This is true for a knife, which, in the hand of a surgeon, can save a life. In the hand of a killer, a knife can take a life.

It's the thinking behind the action that makes the difference. This is what Shakespeare meant in his famous quotation above: *"There is nothing either good or bad, but thinking makes it so."*

The 7 Principles of Influence are like that, too. The attitude we bring to the table is everything.

We will mainly focus on the positive side of influence. However, we'll also look briefly at the dark side, which is a bit like the dark net of manipulation. Monsters "lurk in the dark net" to trip us up and lead us in the wrong direction.

The Forbes Research

A Forbes report from 2024 showed the key management skills needed for effectiveness at work.

Two areas which were always in the top 4 as being the most important for managers are: **Great persuasion** and **excellent presentation** skills.

THE FORBES SURVEY

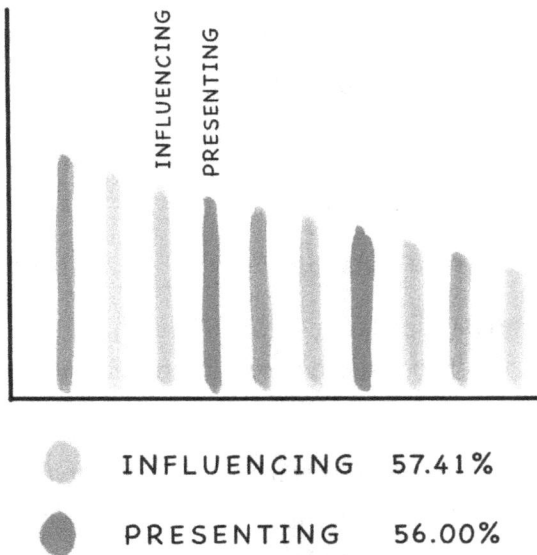

INFLUENCING

PRESENTING

INFLUENCING   57.41%

PRESENTING   56.00%

When I discovered how valuable these two fields are, "Influence and Presenting," I decided to create a unique combination of the two.

In this chapter, I draw back the curtain on just three of the seven principles of influence specifically for international presenters.

Ethical Influence

Before we go on to introduce Johanna, Andy and Thomas – let's first look briefly at four main ways in which people influence one another. I will cover the dark side of influencing and its dangers as well as the positive side.

4 Options: Influence, Persuasion, Coercion, Manipulation

Which option you choose depends on the attitude, intention and desire you bring to any situation.

The Good Guys

Influence is the ability to affect change without forcing anyone to change their opinion.

Influencing someone means that they make the decision to do something all on their own.

Persuasion is very similar to influence and aims to change someone's thoughts, ideas, or actions through some type of information or reasoning on your part. At the heart of persuading people is convincing people to change their views on the basis of your arguments or approach.

In this chapter, you will learn nine ways to influence your audience positively.

The Bad Guys

Coercion is forcing a person to decide or to do something you want through the use of force or threats. It involves pushing a person to do something that they might not really want to do.

Manipulation is all about control. It's about controlling someone else to the point that you use unscrupulous acts to get what you want.

In this chapter, you will also learn two methods tricksters use to influence their audience negatively.

We will see how three people – Andy, Thomas and Johanna – learn to make powerful and influential presentations as they learn to use three of these seven principles: Authority, Liking and Reciprocity. This seven-step coaching structure was the one used to help these three people. The structure did not change but the content of each section changed depending on the person who I was coaching.

It is sometimes called the Hero's Journey based on the classic work by Joseph Campbell, *The Hero with a Thousand Faces.*

The Plan for our Journey

1. The person

2. Her/his problem

3. A guide comes alongside

4. With a plan

5. Calls them to action

6. Helping them to avoid or overcome failure, and

7. Guiding them to success

12 State-of-the-Art Insider Secrets

How to influence when presenting

In the following three sections, you will see short case studies of three of my clients. You will read how we implemented the principles of Authority, Liking and Reciprocity to their unique presenting challenges.

By the end of this chapter, you will have 11 insider secrets that you can apply to your own presentations. Please follow along as I describe their individual coaching journeys. In joining us on this journey, you will also get practical hands-on, scientifically-proven ways to create better results.

Part 1 - AUTHORITY

Johanna's Coaching Story

1. Let me introduce Johanna

Johanna came to me as I was standing in a room making coffee at a company where I was working as a consultant. She looked a bit nervous.

2. Her problem

While chatting over coffee, she said she was nervous about presenting data to groups of men and women. She wanted to develop good relations with people she didn't know well.

3. Johanna's guide appears

Johanna asked me to coach her to enable her to project authority in her presentation. She wanted these seasoned experts to respect her for her high level of know-how in the customer support field.

4. Make a plan

Johanna and I worked on a plan – a grand design! Then, I demonstrated to her that she needed to learn some special secrets from research on influence. We were going to focus on the area of Authority.

5. Call to action

As in Johanna's and Thomas´sessions, I started our coaching with this question – often called the magical question: "If I waved a magic wand, and the problem was gone and you could influence your audience profoundly, what would be different?" This question is so powerful because it transported Johanna to the realm of possibility.

6. Helping her to avoid or overcome failure

Johanna's three key goals were, firstly, to understand what authority is and why it's important. Secondly, how to demonstrate it – especially if you're younger than the people in the audience. And thirdly, how to gain more confidence when presenting. During our work together, Johanna had some ups and downs but was very determined to complete our work and she kept on track. Her focus was crystal clear.

7. Guiding her to success

The big day was in sight. She was going to have to give her first presentation at a kickoff meeting for a big new project which all her new team would be attending.

The day before the meeting, I called Johanna to wish her luck. In the evening, she got back in touch with me to say she was exhausted but really pleased that the result was great. She'd gotten buy-in from her audience for her new project, and she got the feeling that they liked her and felt that she knew what she was doing. In other words, she felt that they recognised her authority, even though she was still quite young!

Our input sessions

Because Johanna wanted to be more authoritative, let's begin with the Authority Factor. Our series of 12 coaching sessions lasted eight weeks.

Our learning transfer activity involved micro-practice sessions to integrate this new input. We always recorded this and analyzed the short sections.

Authority - 3 Positive Ways of Using Authority and 1 Negative Example

> *"Believe one who has proved it. Believe an expert."*
>
> – Virgil, Aeneid Roman Epic Poet (70 BC – 19 BC)

When speaking, authority comes from being seen as an authority in your field, i.e. you are an expert and are viewed as such by your audience. Alternatively, it could be that you are in a position of authority. For example, you are the boss of the company.

Our goal is to come across as an authority on the topic. It's important to be seen as someone who really knows her/his stuff and can be trusted.

There are many ways in which you can project authority when you are presenting, and here I will mention 3 of them.

1. Dress

- *"Dress for success."*

As a general guide, the most successful people tend to wear the most elegant suits and ties.

There are exceptions, of course. For example, people refer to Steve Jobs who came out on stage in these jeans and T-shirts. But Jobs was an idol to many people and was renowned the world over.

In a nutshell, research has shown that people are more willing to follow people who are well-dressed than those who are not.

2. Posture/Breathing/Voice

- *"It is not what you say but the way that you say it."*

Margaret Thatcher, the former prime minister of the UK, had a problem. Her extremely high-pitched voice had a huge negative effect on her authority. So, she got a coach to train her to develop a deeper tone of voice.

Body language also plays a huge factor, especially when you're standing on stage. It's important that the hands and the voice work in synchrony and are not viewed as separate parts. They need to work as a team, as this makes the presenter look more natural and at ease.

3. Do not introduce yourself

Ask someone else to introduce you!

Saying how great you are and showing off is not a great way to demonstrate your authority. This is especially so if you're British and will be frowned upon in most circles, especially in circles where people have high qualifications.

Even if you have the highest educational achievements in the UK, we don't go about saying how many doctorates we've earned. In other cultures, people often write a huge string of letters after their name to demonstrate how accomplished they are. Don't do this in the UK; it will work against you. Make sure you get a qualified person to introduce you.

Key Takeaway

Confidence is important in demonstrating authority.

Confidence comes from knowing what you want to say. This comes through practice and repetition. Practice often and efficiently. Stephen Covey called this constant practice, "sharpening the saw".

Part 2 - LIKING

Thomas's coaching story

1. Let me introduce Thomas
Thomas came to me as I was sitting in a room where I was running a meeting. I was having a 10-minute break.

2. His problem
I knew Thomas quite well because he had taken part in some events I organised as a consultant. He explained to me that he was in line to become a regional sales manager.

3. Thomas's guide appears
Thomas asked me if I'd be prepared to help him in this. And I agreed.

4. We made a plan
Thomas and I worked on a plan. And I showed him that there was some interesting research about the leverage that managers get by using Dr Cialdini's 7 Principles of Influence.

In our plan, I showed him a couple of examples of Liking and why it's so important both in business and specifically when you are presenting to groups.

5. Call to action
As in Johanna's session, I started our coaching with this question – often called the magical question: "If I waved a magic wand, and the problem was gone, and you could influence your audience profoundly, what would be different?" This question is so powerful because it transported Thomas to the realm of possibility.

Thomas wanted to be able to learn some practical insider secrets for developing a quick relationship with people, based on sincerity and not trickery.

6. Helping Thomas to avoid or overcome failure
Thomas wanted to iron out his tendency to use very direct, rude-sounding ways of speaking. This came from his native language, German, which is a very direct language.

7. Guiding him to success
We stuck to our plan of introducing micro units of input. These were usually 20 minutes long and then we moved to the practice phase, again for 20 minutes. So, we alternated between input, practice input, practice, etc.

Thomas soon got the new job with a 10,000 Euro higher annual salary.

Our input sessions

We began our exploration by talking about three ways in which we can bring across feelings of Liking to our audience and started with some key insights based on the latest research.

Liking - 3 Positive Ways to use Liking and 1 Negative Example

"All things being equal, people do business (and other stuff) with friends. All things being unequal, people still do business with friends (and other stuff) with friends. So make friends!"

– Mark McCormack
(marketer to sporting greats like Jack Nicklaus, the famous golfer)

Liking is a universal tendency that is programmed within all human beings. Our ancestors needed mutual liking so that members of our tribe would help each other in difficult situations. And we depend on our "tribes" just as much as our ancestors did.

There are three main aspects of liking. We like people who are similar to us. We like people who pay us real compliments. We also like people who are physically attractive. In other words, we assign likeable traits to attractive people.

When we speak professionally, we project Liking by:

- Showing that we have the audiences' best interests at heart. We are not just there to get their money!

- By providing real and useful value the audience can use to improve their lives.

When we speak, Liking has a huge impact on whether people react positively to us and to our message. There are many ways we can do this. We want to influence two aspects.

Firstly, the atmosphere in the room, the feeling that you really want to help the audience. And secondly, to create a willingness to accept new ideas. This could result in an outcome like a new sale or a new long-term business supplier.

Some ways to show liking

The Smile

Smiles are important because they are built into our DNA as a fair signal of willingness to be a friend. Friends were especially important for survival in the prehistoric environment. You could argue that friends are even more important now that we're bombarded by thousands of negative messages a day. Companies also realise the importance of a smile and they incorporate it into their logos. This includes really big names like Amazon.

Making Contact

Make contact with people before the talk (e.g. via LinkedIn) and send them something useful. This makes your audience members feel special. They will not see you as a stranger but as an ally.

Uncover Commonalities

Look for things you have in common. e.g. hobbies, travel, sport, golf, red wine, chocolate, movies. You can do this by asking open and inquisitive questions. Just be really interested in the people you speak to. Send a real message.

Here are three ways to do that:

- The very best message would be a real card in a real envelope with a real stamp on it. Address it personally and thank the person for coming.

- The next best option would be to send a personalised thank you email.

- And I have kept the best until last! If you really want to make a really big impression then send a personalised present based on some commonality you have discovered by corresponding with this person. This would be the Gold Star of gift-giving – the best option. However, it takes thought and some time to get to know the person. When you are ready, then give it from the heart.

The Dark Side of Liking

False affiliation

I've seen some salespeople try to manipulate others by falsely affiliating themselves with influential groups or individuals.

Key Takeaway

Genuine Interest

We demonstrate likeability by being interested in people. Likeability does not occur by trying to impress them.

Part 3 - RECIPROCITY

Andy's coaching story

1. Let me introduce Andy

I had known Andy for quite a long time because he had started as a young apprentice at the international company where I was working as a trainer.

2. His problem

After he'd been at the company for about 10 years, he was promoted to a junior management position. And ten years after that, he was keen to get a promotion.

3. Andy's guide appears

Andy asked me if I could help him to do this. And I explained a few things about the state-of-the-art research on persuasion and influencing, especially in relation to the Reciprocity factor.

So, Andy asked me if I could support him in getting a management job which would make him the leader of 35 people.

4. Make a plan
We decided how we wanted to work together and set up a plan and timetable so that we could tick off key milestones on our progress chart.

5. Call to action
As in Johanna's and Thomas´ sessions, I started our coaching with this question – often called the magical question: "If I waved a magic wand, and the problem was gone and you could influence your audience profoundly, what would be different?" This question is so powerful because it transported Andy to the realm of possibility.

6. Helping him to avoid or overcome failure
Andy wanted to move forward fast. To do this, he needed to understand reciprocity and how to use it ethically.

7. Guiding him to success
He quickly saw how reciprocity really does help to create great rapport quickly. Andy and I set up a clear plan as to how he could systematically nurture his contacts.

In the end, Andy got the job, and about a year and a half later, he moved to a higher position in another company. He was really pleased with the results. He also got a much higher salary – 15,000 Euro more per year than at his previous company.

Our input sessions

Andy had some great insights into Reciprocity. These sessions were short and were interspersed with short videos where I showed best practices of well-known speakers.

We started by discussing three ways to convey feelings of Reciprocity to our audience, starting with some key insights based on the latest research.

Reciprocity - 3 Positive Ways of Using Reciprocity and 1 Negative Example

"All societies subscribe to the rule of giving and receiving (Reciprocity)"

– Alvin Guldner

Richard Leakey explains that the essence of what makes us human has to do with the system of giving and receiving. Giving and receiving was a way in which humans could support one another by exchanging goods.

How do we define reciprocity?
Reciprocity is an inbuilt human tendency to want to repay in kind. If I receive something from someone, then I want to give them something in return.

How do we project reciprocity when we speak professionally?
In presenting, there is a continual give and take of various aspects.

Two key questions are:

- Do you really listen to your audience in eliciting their needs?

- Do you give them your full attention without having a hidden agenda?

Some ways to show Reciprocity

1. Insider secrets
Give insider secrets related to your topic. This will make your audience feel privileged and more willing to reciprocate by really engaging with your presentation.

2. Send thank you notes
Follow up with personalised thank you notes. Why use this? This simple gesture strengthens the bond between you and your audience and encourages them to "give back to you" in the future.

3. Give your attention

As a thank you for people coming to your presentation or meeting, give them the gift of your full attention. This is the most valuable gift you can give.

The Dark Side of Reciprocity

"Now you owe me one!"

– Dr Cialdini, commenting on what NOT to say

Deceptive charity tactics

You pretend to support a charity so that people are open to showing you goodwill. However, you never actually donate to the charity which you tell your audience you support.

Key Takeaway

Give gifts sensitively and think about them carefully. Give quality gifts.

The Magic of Influence

Now that you are at the end of this short chapter, and here is some "food for thought" by Arthur C Clarke:

> *"Any sufficiently advanced technology is*
> *indistinguishable from magic."*
>
> – Arthur C. Clarke

This quotation is relevant when we speak about influence. We are often puzzled by how some people appear to almost magically get what they want. Not only this, but they also help others to get what they want too.

Other people are unable to inspire change in their business partners, bosses, audience members or family. They have no influence on them and they do not change their behaviour.

What appears to be magical is in fact easy to explain. The truly skilled practitioner of influence has studied and internalised a set of powerful and persuasive tools which encourage change in their audience.

James Rose

Cialdini Certified Coach in Ethical Persuasion – Trainer, Speaker and Business Coach

ABOUT THE AUTHOR: JAMES ROSE

James Rose is one of the UK's most accomplished and experienced communication skills experts. As a member of the Cialdini Institute in the UK, he became one of the first people globally to qualify as a Certified Cialdini Coach. He is a much sought-after trainer, speaker and business coach.

James works across numerous industries, businesses and UK government departments, from front-line staff to C-suite business leaders. He uses research from behavioural science and human psychology, providing unique, practical and powerful ways to maximise the outcome of every business transaction, be that sales and acquisition, customer and client experience or project, staff or stake-holder management.

In his 25-year career, he has worked with clients as varied as HSBC, Volkswagen, Honda, KPMG, Capita, The Foreign and Commonwealth Office, House of Lords, Aviva Insurance and Chelsea Football Club, to name but a few.

Of all the topics on which James trains, speaks and coaches, it continues to be the principles of Influence and Persuasion that learners feel inspired by. Why? Because influence is one of the most important skills needed to be successful in business… but it's rarely, if ever, taught. In fact, recent research cited in Forbes magazine shows that negotiation and persuasion are two of the most sought -after skill requirements for over half of top-paying jobs.

If you want to win more sales, retain more customers and clients, be heard, be respected, earn more, get that promotion and accomplish so much more, you have to be able to influence and persuade those around you.

Imagine if you knew you would achieve excellent results just by strategically choosing the right words at the right time. Imagine the power that would give you!

On a personal note, James is a keen runner and cyclist. He has completed two London Marathons and cycled the length of Great Britain over 12 days (that's over 1000 miles). With these and other accomplishments, he has raised thousands of pounds for his chosen charity, the MS Society.

James is married, with two teenage children, and two dogs.

Contact James at https://www.linkedin.com/in/james-rose-influence-for-success and www.cxpeople.co.uk

CHAPTER 4

Sell without Selling: The Power of Words on Customer Decisions

By James Rose

Twenty years ago, I accepted a job as a Senior Organisation Development Consultant. I didn't apply for the senior part, but apparently did well at the interview!

The problem with being a member of the senior leadership team was that suddenly I was responsible not only for the quality of my work, but also for bringing wealth into the company. Without any experience in sales at this level, or business development, or stakeholder management, I now had a target of bringing in tens of thousands of pounds in new client work.

It was then that my manager gave me the best advice I've ever been given. She said to just, "Be nice, be interested, be helpful."

It's remarkable how powerfully those words affected me. Words are capable of shaping our perceptions, altering our emotions, and ultimately influencing ours and others' decision-making processes. After all, words are magic, that's why we spell them!

Little did I know, she was advising me to follow one of Robert Cialdini's most powerful Principles, the Principle of Liking. Equally, little did I know that these six words would set me on a path towards becoming a member of the Cialdini Institute and also a qualified trainer, speaker and coach of the Principles.

So, who is this chapter for? Everyone involved in any aspect of selling. Many people believe selling is a transaction between someone who we'll call the owner, and someone else who wants to be the future owner. Whether that's ownership of a product, service or knowledge, most salespeople will crudely 'push' what they own (facts, data, details, features) towards the future owner. And this may work, particularly when the future owner really wants what's being offered.

But we're not talking about such a scenario. We're talking about those transactions where there's indecision, lack of attention or motivation to buy, lack of understanding or fear, meaning that what the owner says and does can have a significant impact on the outcome.

I'll give you a series of examples from one recent transaction.

I had cause to give feedback to a retailer. I was mystery shopping the sales experience at a major car brand here in the UK. I made an appointment and showed up on time.

On arrival, the receptionist greeted me with, "Oh, we weren't expecting you today." Six words that completely drained the excitement of test driving a top-of-the-range car and leaving instead feelings of disappointment, frustration and negativity.

During the test drive, the salesperson called me Matthew. One word to break rapport, lower trust and make me dislike him. Which also meant I would have been less inclined to buy from him and his dealership (if this was a real scenario, of course)!

Also during the test drive, we were chatting and football came up. I mentioned I support Arsenal to which he replied, "Why? Terrible team. I hate

Arteta (the manager)." And while this may be true for him, he'd clearly put a barrier between us, creating two warring parties and destroying Unity (the 7th Principle). Only six words, but enough for me to have walked away immediately. Clearly this is not a good strategy to use when selling and yet he had over 15 years' sales experience (he told me more than once!).

I think we can all recognise the poor salesmanship used, when all it would have taken was for him to "Be nice, be interested, be helpful."

In this chapter, we will explore the magical potency of words and how they can sway choices, particularly in business-to-business conversations. Whether you're an out-and-out salesperson or not, once you've read this chapter you will never enter a business conversation the same way again. I'm betting you will choose your words more strategically and recognise the power they have. And if not this, you will want to know more about how to choose the right words, at the right time, to get the best results, helping you hear 'yes' more often!

Why? Because at the heart of how words can influence outcomes lies the art of persuasion. Persuasive language, when used appropriately and ethically, is about effectively communicating ideas and fostering agreement. In business-to-business sales, the ability to persuade is key to your success. When used well, a sales pitch that resonates with potential clients can turn a sceptic into a buyer because it builds trust, overcomes uncertainty and motivates action.

Likewise, when you consciously choose the right words at the right time, you can evoke a spectrum of emotions, from excitement and curiosity to trust and reassurance. Savvy sales professionals understand the importance of emotional appeal in their communication. For instance, a divorce lawyer trying to convert an enquiry call into a paying client may use words like "protect," "secure," and "peace of mind" to evoke feelings of safety and trust.

Speaking of trust, this is another prerequisite for salespeople. Trust is the cornerstone of any successful business relationship and words can either reinforce or undermine it. In the context of business-to-business sales, establishing trust is essential for closing deals. In my car example earlier, when told they weren't expecting me, it broke trust and had me on edge for the rest of the visit. My first impression negatively coloured the rest of the experience, making me look for and therefore find the worst aspects of their salesmanship.

How about this example of words influencing outcomes. Have you ever been shopping for something specific, maybe new furniture for a bedroom, and the store selling the items you like has a sign in the window saying, 'Sale ends tomorrow'? Chances are, those three words will prompt you to buy sooner than you might otherwise have done. Marketeers have known for years how the Scarcity Principle can speed up the decision-making process and lead to quicker conversions.

So, let me ask you a question. When you have to sell your products, services, or advice, do you prefer to push the customer or client towards the sale using heavy-handed tactics or do you prefer to pull them towards you and your offer, drawing people in willingly? Let's put some research behind this...

A study by Johnson-Boyd and Zawisza in 2012 examined customer responses to different persuasion techniques in advertising. They found that strategies that emphasised empowerment and autonomy, such as providing information and allowing customers to make their own choices, were received more positively and shown to be more effective in influencing the customer's decision to buy compared to tactics that were thought to be more coercive or manipulative and pushy.

In 2018, research by Purnawirawan et al looked at the impact of influence tactics on buyer behaviour in the online world. They found that strategies such as Social Proof, where customers see others endorsing a product or service are highly influential in determining whether the customer went on to purchase or not. Their work suggests that people are far more receptive to influence from people they see as like themselves rather than feeling pressured by someone they may have difficulty trusting, like a pushy salesperson.

Finally, 2020 research by Park and Kim looked at the role of trust in customer decision-making, specifically in online environments. They found that the degree to which a customer felt they could trust the seller positively influenced their purchasing decision, which means providing transparent information and guarantees was more effective than pushy sales tactics.

Many other studies show the same results: people generally prefer to be influenced rather than pushed into making their purchases. This is the same for business-to-business interactions and business-to-consumer interactions. Influence strategies that respect the individual's autonomy and focus on building trust and understanding are far more effective.

So, what does it boil down to? Be nice, be interested, be helpful. And demonstrate these three qualities by consciously and strategically choosing your words. The next question is, how?

A year ago, I was asked by a law firm client if I could help them with their client acquisition and retention strategy. As with many law firms, they had promoted some of their more junior legal advisors into more senior roles but not given them training in how to bring wealth to their firm. Instead, they relied on more senior team members to act as role models.

My first two steps were to mystery shop their processes and actions and then conduct group and 1-2-1 feedback sessions. To summarise, the results showed a large degree of passion and engagement, but a low degree of capability in business development. Not only did team members not know how to influence the outcomes of their conversations, but they were typically low in confidence when it came to 'selling' their advice, products and services. Too often, this meant prospective and existing clients would go to other law firms for their legal advice.

The firm I was working with were literally giving business to their competitors simply because they either couldn't, or didn't know how to sell! That's crazy, right?

So, how did I help people who were low on confidence and skills learn how to sell without selling?

Step 1 in any transaction is to build rapport, trust and likeability. Without this foundation, it doesn't matter what you say as the prospect is less likely to listen to you, believe you, or follow your advice.

To build liking, I advised our law firm team members to think of it as a summer holiday. Just because it's sunny doesn't mean you'll love your time away. There are lots of factors, like the hotel, the nightlife, the people, the food and drink and so on. It's the same with liking – you have to manage various moments in your client's experience.

I advised the firm to update their website with a welcoming message so that clients landing on their home page were more likely to 'like' their firm, especially compared to their competitors' more corporate look. They quickly incorporated a simple 'Welcome to (firm name) and thank you for visiting our website' message on the home page. One sentence that creates a feeling of warmth, openness and approachability.

Next, we overhauled the welcome at their offices. Until this point, the receptionists would be fairly aloof in an attempt to project authority and formality. Which is fine in some circumstances but not for this regional law firm. Instead, we rebranded the term 'Receptionist' to 'Director of First Impressions'. This simple change of words led to a substantial increase in confidence among the team, as well as feelings of empowerment, engagement and enthusiasm.

Over the next few months, client feedback noted the friendly greeting and helpfulness of the reception team. Not only did this improve the reputation of the firm, but also meant that when the legal advisor needed to 'sell' their services, clients were already feeling positive about the firm and its ability to help them. Essentially, what the reception team were doing was giving the legal advisor a big advantage when selling their advice and services. More later in the chapter…

Let's change tack now. Imagine you're working in a shop and have been tasked with increasing sales. You've no idea how and hate the idea of having to 'sell' and be pushy. Try adding these 3 words next time… 'It's your choice' (or similar depending on context). Research shows that if you give customers the perception of choice, rather than making them feel like you're forcing them into something they may not otherwise chosen to buy, they will be more inclined to accept your suggestion.

A few years ago, my team and I worked with a major UK high-street chain store. Specifically, we worked with their coffee and restaurant concessions – 165 of them across the country. Simply training team members to add 'It's your choice' when offering an upsell or cross-sell (that is, suggesting an additional purchase similar to what's already on their tray), led to an increase of almost £1 million in extra revenue over 6 months (the client's figures, not ours). Three words to make close to £1 million! What could similar tactics do for your business, I wonder?

More recently, I've been working with an Alternative Networks Provider – broadband essentially. Their door-to-door sales teams will knock on doors and tell prospective customers that their product is cheaper, faster and more reliable. Typical sales strategies – push information at the customer and expect them to agree to buy.

However, there are lots of reasons why this doesn't always work, lack of trust being uppermost. I don't know about you, but if a stranger knocks on my door, I'm instantly on the defensive and not inclined to believe what they say, even if they can offer facts and data to back up their claims.

So, what should they be saying to build trust within a short space of time, so that when they do lay out the facts, data and benefits, the prospect will be more inclined to listen and act?

It's like baking a cake. You need lots of ingredients, which you mix into the bowl before placing it in the oven. So, what are the ingredients for building trust first so that the prospect listens to the facts, data and benefits after?

Step 1 is mindset. Even if the previous attempt at selling hasn't gone well, it's important to shake it off. I often liken it to the old Superman programmes from the 1970s, where Clark Kent goes into the telephone box dressed as a mild-mannered journalist, spins around and comes out in his Lycra outfit and wearing his underwear on the outside of his tights! As someone responsible for selling, it's the same process. Shake off the 'old you', the one that just failed to make the sale, and believe in yourself and your capability for the next attempt. Every time. Because at the end of the day, whether you tell yourself you can or you can't, you're right!

Now imagine the prospect peeks out from behind their curtains ('drapes' in the US) and sees the salesperson walking up their driveway. What do you want them to see? This will vary by situation but typically includes smart clothes, polished shoes, and body language that is confident and welcoming. Essentially the prospect needs to think positive thoughts at this stage.

The next ingredient in building trust is your first words. The door opens. What do you say? For this sales team, it was typically to introduce themselves by name and state why they were there. Which is fine but doesn't influence the potentially defensive customer to listen and engage.

In our training workshops, we encouraged the team to continue to state their name but follow up with a (genuine) compliment whenever possible. By the end of the development programme, the consensus was that the favourite compliment to offer was on someone's slippers, closely followed by their front garden. Fun slippers or well-tended gardens are easy to compliment as they appeal to people's sense of humour or achievement.

In business-to-business transactions, other compliments can include their bag, glasses, tie, shoes, their decision to talk to you, good time keeping, taking the first step and so on.

Coupling this with a degree of Social Proof led to excellent results for the sales team's ability to spark up conversation and build Liking. Mentioning others in the area who had benefitted from a conversation about internet use worked wonders. For example, mentioning that your Ring doorbell relies on higher upload speed to notify you of someone at the door and without this, you may miss that all-important delivery! Just saying, "I spoke to X in your street, and she has decided to use our services simply because…" was a real winner for our team.

Even better, get someone else to add the Social Proof for you. Look for ways your colleagues at work can "talk you up". Maybe it's a colleague who transfers a call to you, or your boss who introduces you at the start of the meeting. The more they can say good things about you, for example, "I'll transfer you to my colleague, X. (S)he is lovely and a real expert in (what the customer needs)", the further ahead of the start line you'll be and the more chance you have of positively influencing the outcome of the conversation you're about to have!

By way of an example, I recently delivered a presentation to 450 people on the Cialdini Principles and their effectiveness in increasing authority without hierarchy (think graduates in high-responsibility roles).

Before being welcomed on stage, I handed the MC a note asking him to "Please use the following words when introducing me", which he did. I had instant authority and the audience, even before I spoke, was invested, engaged, more positive, listened harder, accepted my message more readily and retained more information. Of course, I can't guarantee it was all due to the strong introduction, but I'm confident this played a significant part.

And if you're wondering, my introduction was….

"Now I'd like to introduce James Rose to the stage. James is an expert in influencing skills, having worked with hundreds of businesses and organisations like ours. He is a member of the Cialdini Institute in the UK and one of only a handful of qualified practitioners globally. James has worked with some of the biggest brands in the world, including HSBC, Honda, Volkswagen, the Ministry of Defence and KPMG to name but a few. We are incredibly lucky to have him with us today, so please join me in welcoming James to the stage".

In just a few dozen words, I have hit the audience with Social Proof, Authority, Liking and Scarcity!

This brings us nicely back to our law firm friends. As you'll remember, we've already changed the greeting on their website and how the Director of First Impressions manages the client upon arrival at the office. So now, let's turn our attention to the legal advisors. How can someone in a role which really isn't a sales role bring substantial amounts of wealth into their firm?

By now, you should know how they should greet their client – with a compliment. Before I worked with them, they were all business and no small talk. Particularly in Western cultures, we like to settle in first, so a bit of chit-chat is essential for building trust and making the "sale" easier. I encouraged the legal advisors not only to compliment the client, but also to find similarities such as the age of kids, where they grew up, common hobbies and interests and so on. Of course, as with all attempts to influence, it must be done ethically and authentically, but simply pointing out that "we're like each other" is a useful way to settle the client and help them feel safe—which, of course, is a powerful way to build trust.

As is often the way with experts, they are keen to divulge their expertise in an attempt to impress the prospect. However, for our legal advisors, we encouraged them to ask lots of questions first. Why? Being interested isn't just about the answers to the questions. It's about showing you value the client, care about them and their needs. It makes them feel listened to and therefore valued, and of course, will subsequently help offer the right advice in a tailored way.

This simple switch was groundbreaking for the team. They went from being just another firm of lawyers to trusted advisors. Over the next few months, not only did they convert more enquiring prospects into fee-paying clients, but they retained their clients by offering additional services in other practice areas and also gained more referrals from existing clients.

Knowing how to influence is one of the least-trained skills in business, but it's also one of the most powerful ways to achieve success. There are so many ways to ensure you achieve everything you're capable of, and effective use of the Cialdini Principles is an excellent way to start. After all, if it's good enough for Warren Buffet, Richard Branson and Guy Kawasaki, it's got to be good enough for the rest of us, right?

And if you're wondering where to start, how about "be nice, be interested, be helpful."

It's not rocket science by any means, but it could skyrocket your sales!

Martin John
Cialdini Certified Coach in Ethical Persuasion, Procurement
Expert, Trainer, Coach

ABOUT THE AUTHOR: MARTIN JOHN

Welsh-born Martin John is a Procurement expert, trainer and speaker, now living in the south of England.

Across a 26-year career, he held senior management roles within Procurement and Supply Chain at leading global companies, such as Toyota Motor Manufacturing, Rexam Packaging and British American Tobacco.

His live online and in-person training courses see him impart his unique blend of technical expertise, focus on practical application, unparalleled engagement and strong sense of fun on his delegates.

Aside from Procurement topics, Martin's specialties are negotiation and persuasion, and he considers these essential skills for life, not just work.

Yet many people lack the confidence and knowledge to negotiate effectively and don't know how to hear "yes" more often through following scientifically proven influence techniques.

This is true for even some of the largest corporations with whom he works.

He teaches Procurement and Sales teams the tools and techniques to negotiate consciously and competently, getting better deals and leaving less value on the negotiating table.

As a Cialdini Certified Coach, Martin also teaches Dr Robert Cialdini's 7 Principles of Persuasion and crucially, how to practically apply them, helping others grow their influence to achieve greater business success.

Martin has five Procurement courses on the biggest business-learning platform in the world, LinkedIn Learning, plus courses on Udemy.com that have been taken by thousands of people all over the world. He's also delivered live training to companies across Europe, US, Australasia and the Middle East.

He is a public speaker and has appeared on several podcasts, including co-hosting the "Demystifying Procurement" podcast, where he and his fellow co-hosts cut through the jargon to help junior Procurement practitioners thrive.

Martin is an avid reader of all things negotiation and the application of behavioural science, and is a frequent LinkedIn contributor on these topics, sharing what he's learned, sprinkled liberally with his sense of humor.

He is married with 2 children, who, at the time of writing, stubbornly remain on the payroll. He loves keeping fit, horseracing, sailing, and he also plays the bass guitar (to a very mediocre standard).

CHAPTER 5

The Persuasion Edge: Influence in Procurement and Purchasing

By Martin John

Trigger warning: What you're about to read may be unsettling. You'll be learning about an area of business that you may think should remain hidden in the darkest recesses of the internet, or in speciality bookstores. Rest easy. I want to bring the power of applying ethical influence in Procurement and Purchasing out of the shadows, into plain sight. You'll thank me.

Note: I use the terms "Purchasing" and "Procurement" interchangeably, even though to the pedants among this fraternity (er, that includes me) there IS a difference.

What the heck is Purchasing anyhow, and why is it important to businesses?

For those of you unfamiliar with what Purchasing does, let me give you some examples (and don't worry if you're a member of the vast majority of humanity that doesn't know this, I won't take offence).

Think about a car manufacturer and a hospital.

The car manufacturer will need to buy thousands of different components like tyres, lights and windshields from many different suppliers, and then bring them all together to assemble a vehicle. They might also buy services like advertising or legal advice, too.

Similarly, the hospital will need to buy medical equipment and drugs, as well as cleaning and IT services, etc, so it can operate.

As you can imagine, the sums of money these entities spend on these goods and services will be significant. When spending so much money, the manufacturer and hospital need to ensure they're getting what they agreed to in terms of price, quality, service, reliability and much more, from the suppliers of those goods and services.

It's the job of the Purchasing team to negotiate and manage these often multi-million dollar contracts, securing the best value for the organisation.

Beyond the deals, though, just as important is managing the relationship with 2 key groups.

On the one hand you have the internal stakeholders (colleagues) who are the ones who specify and ultimately use the good or service. From experience, this group can be more challenging because they can choose to ignore or work around Procurement.

On the other hand, there are the salespeople who represent the suppliers that provide the goods and services. Procurement needs to make sure everything works smoothly during a trading relationship which is typically long-term.

Suppliers can be more receptive to your influence because it's in their interests to cultivate a strong relationship with you and your company, so they can ultimately grow revenue.

You can probably now see that a job in Procurement comes with a lot of responsibility.

More than that, with Procurement dealing with so many different people inside and outside of the company, there's also a huge opportunity AND a necessity to apply ethical influence techniques to persuade others to move in your direction.

How much more successful as a Procurement pro could you be if you were to learn how to crack this code? Spoiler alert: you'll find out if you read on.

Why does Sales have the edge over Procurement in the influence stakes?

For every seller, you need a buyer. It's part of the wonderful symmetry of business.

But that's where the symmetry ends. Maybe it's my insecurities, but I think salespeople have a distinct advantage.

Walk into any bookstore or search online and you'll see thousands of titles on sales topics, but you'll be lucky to find anything on Procurement, and quite likely, any texts will be stocked in an obscure and dusty corner of the retailer's premises or website.

Sales folks also benefit from up to 10x more training than their poor relations in Purchasing, too.

So, on the face of things, salespeople appear to have the gift of huge advantage over their buyer counterparts.

But it doesn't need to be like this, does it? And I'd strongly assert that it *shouldn't* be like this.

This is because people buy from, and negotiate with other people, not corporations. The great news is that most human beings, including those of us in Purchasing, are just as capable of learning and applying ethical persuasion techniques as anyone else.

Citing real-life examples from throughout my career, I'm going to show you how, by using the universal principles of ethical persuasion, you can neutralize or, even better, wrest control of the influence agenda to give you an advantage and get more people to say "yes".

Stories from the front line - ethical influence successes

Beginning With The End In Mind - Pre-suasion

How can you "smooth the path" of implementing a change (especially when the change is bad news)?

I'll let you into a little secret here. There's an effective technique sales-people use effortlessly that seems unknown or little practiced by the Pro-curement community. This technique is "conditioning".

It has its roots in "pre-suasion" – a technique used to prepare the other party for an upcoming change (typically bad news) so it doesn't take them by surprise and they become receptive to its inevitable reality.

Buyers face this all the time. Our well-trained sales counterparts drip-feed us news of upcoming price increases, capacity constraints, or changes to service levels into every discussion. This is "buyer conditioning".

But buyers typically aren't very good at "supplier conditioning" and this is a wasted opportunity.

Every supplier interaction is an opportunity to use conditioning in some way, and this technique can be amplified if your colleagues in other depart-ments are also giving the supplier the same message. This takes unflinch-ing internal alignment, but this united front approach can be omnipotent.

It could be that your company is seeking profit improvement, in which case the conditioning message might be "we're under pressure to deliver x% cost savings this year", or supplier performance improvement, "the new Ops Director wants us to remove the bottom-performing suppliers", but it could be anything.

The conditioning message and variations of it, should be delivered to the supplier at every opportunity. To be ethical, the conditioning message should be based on a genuine need.

After suffering year-on-year price increases on one of the commodities I was once managing, I wanted to take control of the conditioning narrative.

Months before contract renewal discussions, my sales counterparts trotted out their usual pre-contract-renewal spiel about labour, energy and transport cost increases and fully expected to get my agreement on yet another sales price increase.

But this time, they also received some conditioning of their very own from me, and from my colleagues in our factories.

The message that was delivered (and paraphrased in various forms) across multiple channels and many meetings was as follows:

"These are challenging times. Our profitability is under pressure and each of our important suppliers is expected to make their contribution. It may need us to take some difficult decisions, but it's in the long-term interest of both parties. A price increase, as you've enjoyed in previous years, isn't going to work."

This put my company in the driver's seat. We had seized the narrative from the suppliers.

By the time I made my requirements explicit during my contract renewal discussions, supplier expectations were well and truly managed. Some still tried to push an increase through, but with the overwhelming effect of the systematic conditioning from our recent interactions, the suppliers really weren't in a strong position.

In the worst case, suppliers agreed to keep prices as they were, but in the best cases, suppliers passed-on price reductions— results that had previously seemed impossible to deliver.

It just goes to show that what you tell them before you try to persuade them is just as important as the persuasion message itself.

Postscript 1: What do you think about the ethical aspects of this approach? As with applying any of the influence principles, they can be abused, and people manipulated.

Aside from basing the conditioning message on a legitimate require-ment, if you're going to be making a change at some point in the future (which will be perceived as bad news for the other party) conditioning is a way of protecting your relationship. The change won't come as a total shock, so the likelihood of histrionics, table-banging, and a damaged relationship is reduced.

Postscript 2: Here's a wonderful example of supplier conditioning from a big retailer you may have heard of, Walmart. Take a look at what's written on the badges that the Procurement executives hand out to visiting suppliers. Wow. Which supplier would want to deny people to live better?

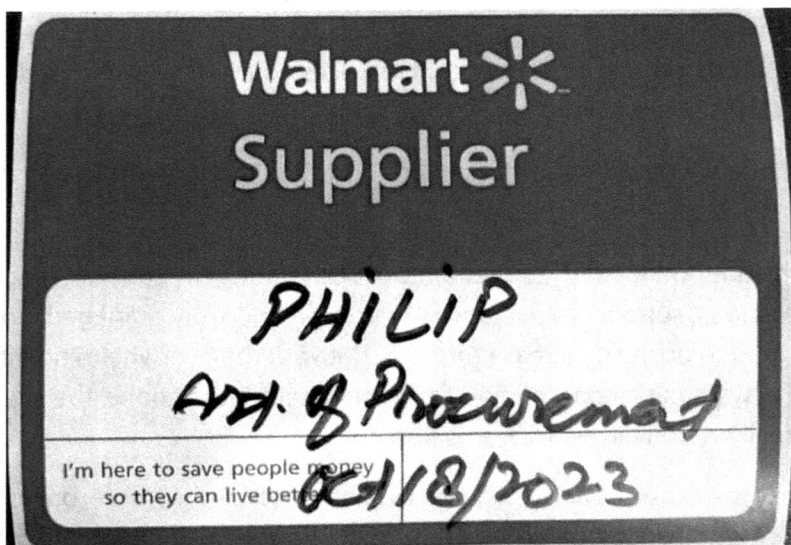

Winning over the doubters and haters – Liking and Reciprocity

I once held a role with the title, "Head of Relationship". Seriously. It had nothing to do with marriage counselling, but everything to do with establishing, growing and maintaining collaborative relationships between Procurement and the rest of the business, principally Marketing, Manufacturing and Finance teams.

Now, during the hiring process, it would have been helpful for me to know that the "rest of the business" absolutely hated Procurement. They treated my function with utter contempt and disdain.

As the "face of Procurement" to the rest of the business, I spent my early days in the role getting shouted at, bullied and was generally used as a metaphorical punchbag.

When I delivered good news, no one cared. When I delivered bad news, the wild dogs were unleashed. It was a most unpleasant experience, shall we say.

If I was going to survive, I would need to cultivate functioning relationships with my stakeholders.

What could I possibly do to soothe the seething masses that would help me develop such a relationship?

Enter stage left, the principles of Reciprocity and Liking. My saviors.

Reciprocity was activated through the provision of intangible gifts.

I listened to my stakeholders intently, then listened some more. I allowed them to vent their frustrations, demonstrating empathy for their situation. For once, it seemed, they felt heard.

I offered valuable advice, such as how they could best navigate the labyrinthine Procurement process (a process seemingly designed to prevent *anyone* from buying *anything*).

I provided unsolicited market and supplier updates, such as raw material availability and pricing information, details of upcoming supplier innovation and suggestions on how they could make their business unit more profitable.

In parallel, I strived to activate the Liking principle. I recognised that I would have to genuinely like the other person first, adopting a mindset of advocating for them and trying to help them, before they could like me.

I must confess, this took some mental flexibility to adopt, given that I was often met with open hostility!

Nevertheless, I sought *similarities* with my sparring partners and was amazed at what I uncovered.

With the main bully, I found that we both loved Indian curry; with a belligerent business leader, I discovered that we both had a passion for horses; and with one of the most anti-Procurement people I'd ever met, the Head of Manufacturing, I uncovered that years earlier we had both worked at the same company.

The sense of a growing connection and cessation of hostilities with these people was palpable. Raising our similarities to awareness and talking about them prior to getting down to business was the key to elevating our relationship.

Now, I'm not saying for one minute that the result was perfect, and of course, there were bumps in the road, but through using 2 powerful principles of influence, not only was the relationship between the business and Procurement repaired, the stakeholders also began to trust me and listen to me.

Eventually, my interactions became pleasant, to the extent that the relationship became sustainable.

What can you do if you find yourself in a situation?

Take a step back and focus on how you can get the foundations of your relationship on the right footing. Take your time to build rapport and gain trust. By using the principles of Liking and Reciprocity, you too will convert the naysayers.

Everyone else is doing it - Social Proof

I once took on a new role and with it came a new boss who was an absolute tyrant. He was a diminutive Brazilian, but whose presence and power belied his 5 foot 3 inch stature.

He would ask THE most laser-focused questions, often ones that I hadn't thought of, and was the most driven and challenging person I've worked for. He struck absolute fear into most of the team he led, and also with those over whom he had no hierarchical control!

I wasn't based in the same office as him (thankfully), but I met him every month for a "catch-up" (which sounds innocuous, but it felt closer to an interrogation). I always went into these meetings expecting to be fired on the spot.

The category I managed was Production Machinery – I bought the machines that made the products my company sold. The annual spend of £250mn was significant, yet it was regarded by my Procurement leaders as having very few opportunities from a cost and cash flow improvement perspective.

It was considered a category that the category manager simply "occupied" just before they were ejected from the business. What a confidence booster!

I was expecting my boss to test me to the extreme, and I didn't have to wait long before I received my first challenge.

Bear in mind that this category wasn't new. The supply market was heavily consolidated, supply capacity was limited, supplier relationships were long-standing. On the other hand, my predecessor hadn't been commercially-minded and had let the suppliers dictate commercial matters for more than 10 years. Suppliers were very comfortable with the status quo.

But my manager wanted to see how he could shake this category up. He demanded that I make a significant contribution to the company's cash flow targets by improving payment terms from the current 30-day terms to 90-day terms.

What were my options? How could I possibly instigate this magnitude of change with suppliers who knew they held the balance of power? Failure certainly wasn't one of my options, given that I wanted to protect my career and continue paying my mortgage.

Turning to the principles of influence, I enlisted the principle of Social Proof. I needed to build a picture of the practices of many "similar others"; the key to being able to benefit from this principle.

What were the typical payment terms of other companies in the production machinery arena, and other similar companies within my supplier's industry sector?

I read dozens of articles, spoke with peers outside of my industry to compare notes, and read the supplier's financial reports and the terms that they applied to *their* suppliers.

With my non-competing peers already enjoying payment terms of 90 days, I established that it was the *de facto* standard across the category. A quick website review also showed that my suppliers paid *their* suppliers on 90-day terms, too!

This was the genesis of my social proof lever.

Strategically selecting the first supplier to target; the market leader and with whom I had the best relationship, I legitimately and ethically asserted that "naturally, I'd like to align payment terms to the industry-standard and to those in which you pay your suppliers."

They accepted. Unleashing the full power of social proof by informing other suppliers that their competitors, within the exact same industry segment, had already agreed to the new terms, worked like a charm.

One by one the dominoes fell, with little further effort from me other than the reminder of social proof; their peers had already agreed.

My target was achieved, my boss was happy / less dissatisfied, and I wasn't fired!

How can you harness this principle? Firstly, it's versatile. Think about any behaviour, contractual term or practice that you'd like your suppliers to adopt.

Choose your first "data point" of social proof strategically (aim for suppliers similar to the one you're trying to influence). The principle then fuels itself the more "similar others" you can persuade.

Find me a better supplier – Consistency

The person I'm going to highlight in this example shares some similarities with my "tyrant" boss from earlier. Short in stature but a hugely influential figure in the business. The main difference though was one of character; he was a very decent human being.

"Rahul" was the Senior VP of Engineering and Manufacturing. He'd been in the industry all his life and had forgotten more than I, a relative newcomer, would ever know.

The supply market was heavily consolidated, with one supplier having a stranglehold on certain high-value, critical production machinery products.

If you're a Procurement pro reading this, you may be wearily familiar with this kind of situation. Having a limited choice of suppliers and a marketplace characterized by a single dominant player is a very uncomfortable and risky place to be.

The long and short is that the supplier knows they're going to be winning your business, so there's no incentive for them to provide you with favourable commercial terms or to strive for continuous improvement. You want good service? Meh, maybe.

After experiencing another woeful delay on a critical piece of equipment, delaying the start of our production and, in turn, delaying payback on the overall investment, the VP had had enough. "Find me a better supplier" were the explicit instructions he gave to me, in front of his senior project team.

I had been scouring the market for alternative suppliers for several months and I'd been nurturing one supplier that had been waiting in the wings for some time, but had never convinced us to select them.

I'd completed all the legal, regulatory, financial and technical due diligence checks for the new potential supplier (the latter with full support from Rahul's team, who were equally disgruntled with the performance of the current supplier), so we were looking for an opportunity to give them a chance.

A new project was soon announced, and I included the new supplier in the "RFP" (Request for Proposal) bidding process.

Pricing from the new supplier was strongly favourable, but I knew that a price benefit alone wasn't a compelling rationale for awarding them the business.

Technically, the new supplier held an advantage. Their solution would bring us greater efficiency. They also offered an enticing maintenance package, operator training and crucially, an underwritten commitment to meeting our lead time.

Like an enthusiastic puppy, I presented the 2 options to Rahul (the existing, unreliable supplier plus the potential new supplier). This was going to be easy.

I objectively outlined the pros and cons of both options and made my recommendation: we've tried to improve the performance of the existing supplier over a long period of time, and we've failed; it's time to introduce a new supplier.

Naively, I expected Rahul to be ecstatic at this prospect. How wrong I was. You see, while we knew about all the shortcomings of the existing supplier, they were a known entity and we, as a business, had built relationships that were intertwined across many departments and at all levels of each company. "Divorce" could be very difficult for both companies.

Rahul pushed back on my recommendation. His preference was to select the existing supplier, after he had given them a stern talk about the performance he expected.

This was frustrating. If we followed Rahul's suggestion, we'd be effectively rewarding the incumbent supplier's poor performance.

But Rahul was the Senior VP of Manufacturing and Engineering. It was his teams that would be the users of the equipment and Rahul was the ultimate decision-maker.

Then I had a brainwave. I recalled Rahul's challenge to me, "find me a better supplier".

Invoking the principle of Consistency, I reminded Rahul of his statement.

"Rahul, I remember our recent conversation. You said you were so unhappy with the current supplier that you wanted me to find a better one. I believe I have accomplished this, and your team agrees. Will you support this recommendation?"

I could almost feel Rahul's inner torment. He had publicly and voluntarily made the statement that I was to find him a better supplier, but at the prospect of "divorce", he now felt torn on how to proceed.

I'd done my homework and aligned with his team. It didn't take him long to make his decision.

With Rahul wanting to act consistently with what he'd said, in public and by his own volition, this was the overwhelming factor that sealed his vote in favour of the new supplier.

Senior people specifically, are successful because they've backed their own judgement throughout their career. When they've publicly and voluntarily made a statement, they will feel great pressure to act consistently with it.

This is your opportunity to benefit from this powerful principle.

Give yourself the persuasion edge – what you should do next

You can now see how critical influencing skills are to help you succeed in your Procurement career. I help teams all over the world improve their influence, which leads to more success. I can help you, too. Get in touch via my website: www.martinjohn-training.com

Mark Brown
Cialdini Certified Coach in Ethical Persuasion, Behavioural Science
Expert, Coach and CEO

ABOUT THE AUTHOR:
MARK BROWN

Mark is a seasoned professional with over 25 years of experience in Financial Markets, working for global banks in major cities worldwide. His roles evolved from focusing on financial targets to managing and influencing people, leading him to train as an executive coach, where he discovered Dr. Robert Cialdini's seminal work, *Influence*. This was a turning point in his career and led to a degree in Psychology. This shift sparked his passion for helping others achieve their potential.

In 2015, he started looking at how to help clients with their cybersecurity concerns. This is where he honed the application of behavioural science research.

Mark's company, Psybersafe, was born out of a need for effective cybersecurity training for employees. The company's success in helping people adapt their behaviours to be more cyber secure has led him to coach others to apply behavioural science techniques as well as Cialdini's principles of persuasion.

Mark's experience is broad and relatable, having worked in large corporate organisations and small start-ups in very different cultures.

Trust is at the core of Mark's work. Psybersafe's largest client has just signed up for year 4, demonstrating their ability to build long-term, successful relationships. Most of their business comes from recommendations from their clients.

Mark is driven by a desire to share what he has learned to help others be successful. He coaches those who are curious and eager to learn the skills to be more influential in their daily lives.

Mark has applied his behavioural science expertise with European Banks like BNP Paribas Fortis, manufacturers like Toyo Ink, as well as a number of start-ups in the UK, Asia, and Europe. He has been featured in a number of publications like Raconteur, HR Director, Startups, and many others.

Mark holds a BSc in Economics and Finance, a BSc in Psychology from the Open University, UK, and a Master's degree from Thunderbird School of Global Management at ASU. His work is not just about 'what' he does, but the 'why' behind it - a testament to his passion and commitment to positive change.

CHAPTER 6

Winning minds, shifting views: How to overcome defensive decision making

By Mark Brown

"An inability to be guided by a 'healthy fear' of bad consequences is a disastrous flaw."

— Daniel Kahneman, Thinking, Fast and Slow.

"You've got to get these people on board!" was the instruction from my CEO. At the time, I was working for a large bank and had just been tasked with changing the operating model of the whole organisation.

Initially, I loved the challenge – I had seniority, influence and control. But it soon began to dawn on me that my idea of the right thing to do was not the same as my senior colleagues'. The experience I'm about to share with you is about what I learned the hard way, so that you don't have to!

A significant part of the difficulty I experienced in this project was having to tackle "Defensive Decision Making" (see Gigerenzer, 2014). The first reaction of most of the people involved was not "how can this benefit the organisation?" but "Hang on, what's this going to do to me and my business?". That reaction is common, because people are often more likely to put their own interests ahead of the organisation's interests. In fact, it's so common that it's also known as CYA – Cover Your Ass, and is even mentioned as such in research papers (see Artinger et al, 2018).

Rory Sutherland—Vice-chairman of Ogilvy and an advertising industry legend—calls this the Heathrow Effect and provides a clear example. Some years ago, it seemed that personal assistants were reluctant to book their bosses on flights to New York's JFK from London City Airport, rather than from Heathrow Airport, even though Heathrow was further away and more difficult to get to from the centre of London, where most professionals work.

Rory suggested that this was because flying from Heathrow was the standard option, and if anything went wrong, British Airways would get the blame. But if you'd booked your boss from London City and the flight was delayed, they would blame you and not the airline: "Why on earth did you book me from this tiny airport?" This blame avoidant strategy serves to minimise any damage to the decision maker, rather than optimising the outcome.

Decision-making within organisations, whether large or small, is a complex process influenced by a variety of factors that go beyond simple rational analysis. These factors include cognitive biases, heuristics, and subconscious drivers, which can significantly impact the decisions made by employees at all levels. Understanding these influences is crucial for improving decision-making processes and outcomes.

My personal challenge with defensive decision-making

Remember that instruction from my CEO? The bank's balance sheet was stuck, which stopped us from lending enough to meet our targets. There was too little capital available, which impeded our ability to lend.

Thirteen different business units were each demanding more capital to provide loans and facilities to their clients.

The bank had made loans over the years through these different departments, focusing on asset-backed lending (loans backed by property, plant, equipment), agribusiness (lending to farmers), commercial real estate, and lending to retail, for example. These units specialised in lending to their sectors, but almost all capital was allocated to supporting existing loan facilities. And no one wanted to sell their loans to free up capital.

But that's exactly what we needed to do.

My colleagues, the business unit heads, resisted this approach because they would no longer get income from those assets. And, notwithstanding the logic, going from running a business of $20 million in annual income to $15 million didn't look good, even if other metrics showed greater efficiency. Plus, the selling price wasn't always good, as loans had been made when rates were lower, so the loans weren't getting enough interest income to be attractive.

So, my job was to convince these senior colleagues to let my unit manage careful asset disposals, freeing up capital so that we could give them more capital to use. We could make a technically sound and logical case, but that's not always relevant.

This was viewed with considerable suspicion, with business heads variously objecting: "Why should my assets be sold?", "That'll reduce the size of my business," and "My revenues will go down." I was also viewed with suspicion – I was relatively new to the bank, so I was seen as an enemy within, promoting my own agenda.

As an organisation, we led by agreement and consensus – not by telling people what to do. So I needed to get the rest of the senior leadership team to trust me and to see that what I was trying to do was in their interest.

If I was going to get them to listen to me with an open mind, I needed to show them I was on their side. Then, I needed to demonstrate this new approach would be beneficial to them – and by association, the wider organisation. My project team and I spent some time thinking about the individuals involved and how we could work with them individually and as a wider team.

We started by classifying the business unit leaders:

- The die-hards in the 'no way' camp who wanted to control what they saw as their business, their clients, their revenue. There were two people in this group, one of whom was actively against the project and all it involved.
- Their followers – perhaps six other managers.
- Two people were definitely in the "let's hear him out, what we've got now isn't working" camp.
- The final group—"if the CEO thinks this is the right way, let's wait and see"—was probably three people.

You can see there was considerable resistance to overcome in this group. The focus of that resistance was me and two other senior leaders who were working on the project. In effect, we had 13 people on one side of the table, all in various stages of denial and defiance, and three of us on the other side trying to win them over.

So, this was the first issue we needed to tackle. How could we show that we were genuinely on their side? One member of my team suggested we hire a management consultant. This would give us someone external and respected to take on the project. While we would guide and advise him, because he was not a portfolio management expert, he would deliver the ideas, assign responsibilities and set deliverables. This would then allow us to move to the "same side of the table" as our colleagues.

At the time, I had an executive coach to help me work through these challenges – which is where my interest in psychology, behavioural science and Dr. Robert Cialdini's work started. I hadn't read Cialdini at this stage, but we followed what I now coach almost exactly. In fact, when I reflect on this project, I can identify several of the Cialdini principles of persuasion that we used to achieve the right outcome.

The Cialdini principle of Unity states that people are inclined to say "yes" to someone they consider to be one of them. Bringing in a third party to manage the project meant my team and I could move to the same side of the table as everyone else and be accepted as part of the bigger team. We could then work together to develop the structural solutions that would underpin the new way of working. Given that something needed change, together we could influence the outcome to make sure we developed the right solutions.

Then we used the principle of Social Proof: when people are uncertain, they look to others to decide what they should be doing. First, we could identify colleagues at other, highly regarded global banks that had adopted this approach and were enthusiastic about the positive impact.

Secondly, and perhaps more effectively, we began to see what Dr. Cialdini calls "Future Social Proof". When some people in the group started to agree and accept and work with the new ideas, they were advocating the new approach to others. This gave the "undecideds" comfort that the new approach might work and, importantly, benefit them after all. And so, whilst we were still a minority, the trend was in our direction and this helped give the "undecideds" more certainty that perhaps we did have the right approach.

This also leveraged the principle of Authority which states that people look to credible experts and unbiased sources of information. The big global banks had adopted the portfolio management approach to managing their lending assets and capital. My colleagues didn't necessarily need to believe me, but could see what the "big boys" were doing for confirmation.

We also saw the principle of Liking in practice. This principle tells us that others say "yes" to us more when they know we genuinely like them. I consciously worked on developing good, authentic relationships with two or three key colleagues by seeking their help and advice on some of the thornier issues. This developed in to a co-creating relationship, and they willingly became part of the solution. They were then a great help in influencing the others in the group.

I've set out the five steps we followed to get this process off to a positive start.

1. We identified exactly who was in which camp, where the frictions were, who we needed to influence, and where they needed persuading.

2. By encouraging good, open conversations, as opposed to initial adversarial interactions, we were able to identify uncertainties about what was being considered, the possible outcomes, and the impacts.

3. We set about building trusting relationships – Cialdini's principles of reciprocity, liking and unity are all relevant in developing good relationships.

4. We took time to listen, explain, and ask for the unit heads' advice to help us co-create the solutions.

5. The fifth step followed the previous four. As people in the group started to accept the changes, we tapped into "Future Social Proof" – even though we were still a minority, the others could see the direction things were moving in, which helped in reducing uncertainty.

The project was a success. We got the right people on board and gained a consensus about the way forward. However, had I been aware of Cialdini's principles of persuasion at that time and known what I know now – and actively coach other people to do – I could have saved myself and the organisation between three and six months of discussion, wrangling and hard work to get the necessary changes adopted. Instead, I did it the hard way.

My advice to you? Don't do it the hard way! Understanding the principles of persuasion is a small investment that will repay itself many times over, both in your professional and personal life.

Top things to take away

There are elements of this example that you can start to use in practice today. To begin with, how do you know you are facing a defensive decision-making challenge? Here are the three main signs:

1. People are not responding to your offer, even though it is logical and will make a positive difference.

2. You are facing open suspicion or dissension.

3. You know your offer is technically or strategically sound, but are struggling with adoption.

Instead of continuing to stress the need for, or features of, your proposition, try these approaches:

1. **Consider how you can improve the relationships you have with your audience.** How can you build better individual relationships that will lead to authentic and ethical two-way trust? It's Cialdini's principle of Liking: if people know that you like them, they expect you'll do the right thing by them. It generates trust and helps develop a strong relationship.

2. **Accept that there is uncertainty in any decision**. Put yourself in your audience's shoes. What might they be thinking? What could they be worried about? How can you help them overcome these uncertainties? The principles of Social Proof and Authority help in overcoming uncertainty about your proposal.

3. **Do your homework.** If you have things in common with your colleagues or potential clients, bring them up. We know that people are more likely to say "yes" to people they consider one of them; part of their "tribe".

Influential thinking for entrepreneurs

Here is another example of "blame avoidant behaviour" that many of my FinTech clients encounter, and that I've experienced myself as an entrepreneur.

John, a client of mine, runs a start-up selling a software application for banks. It's a very specific application related to managing the risk on complex transactions using data which banks get from regulated entities that settle these transactions. His software improves a bank's ability to use this data and make decisions to optimise its positions. In doing so, the bank can potentially save millions in costs.

When he got his business up and running, John contacted the people he knew in the industry. He was well connected as he'd worked extensively in the field, had chaired industry bodies, and was well-respected.

But after a while, he noticed that the people he contacted were happy to talk to him initially, but reluctant to take the next step – introducing him to the decision makers.

What was holding them back? John knew that many banks were managing data on spreadsheets and would not have the insights he could provide. Surely if his application could save $10 million for an outlay of less than a tenth of that, decision makers would want to see it? And he knew that his contacts agreed with what he was saying.

But logic alone often does not lead to the right outcome.

There are a lot of things that go into what John's ex-colleagues would be weighing up – none of them fitting the rational human being model we learned about in economics – the person who optimises choices and always has the best interests of the shareholder at heart.

In psychology, we talk about the dual processes of thinking: controlled versus automatic or systematic versus heuristic. In the 1960s, psychologist Herbert Simon pointed out the role of emotions in decision-making and coined the term 'satisficing' – making a decision because it is satisfactory, not necessarily because it is the best decision.

Further, Daniel Kahneman and his colleague Amos Tversky showed how we use 'heuristics' or subconscious rules and shortcuts in much of our decision making (See Kahneman, 2011) and turned a lot of economic thinking on its head – Kahneman won the Nobel Prize for Economics on the back of this work. He described these dual processes as System 1 thinking (fast, intuitive, automatic) and System 2 thinking (slow, conscious, logical and evaluative). And System 1 thinking accounts for over 90% of our decision-making.

In short, logical argument alone will not get people to say yes to your perfectly good ideas, products, applications or solutions.

So, what should John do? This is where the Cialdini principles of persuasion come in. John could ask his contacts if there is something holding them back, but will he get a straight answer?

It may be that they don't want to look like a fool in front of their boss, taking something to him or her that might be seen as a waste of time. After all, the boss has a lot of influence over the contact's future – whether he'll get a pay rise, a bonus, or even have a job in the future. John's contact would rather not bother the boss, so saying "no", or avoiding a decision is the easy option and deflects any blame if it turns out to be a no-go idea.

How can we ethically persuade the contact that not only would this not be personally risky for them, but could, in fact, make them look good and potentially make their boss look good too?

We needed to remove some uncertainty and gently nudge the contact in the right direction. As part of our coaching, John and I developed an

action plan based on the Cialdini principles of persuasion. This plan was designed to help him not just delve into the logic and the numbers, but also to develop his relationships and see where the uncertainties lay so that he could address them and get his appointments with the decision makers.

For example, John knew his clients had contracted start-ups in other parts of the organisation. Using the principle of Consistency, he pointed out that hiring small "FinTechs" was consistent with the group's approach to bringing in innovative solutions.

He also created a specific report for his contact, using their data. He gave this to his contact, explaining the work he had done for him, but did not hint or ask for anything in return. This showed how his solution could benefit the company, which was useful to the contact. As we know from BJ Fogg's Behavior Model (Fogg 2020), making things easy for people means they don't need as much motivating or convincing to do what you ask of them.

John had put in some effort for his contact without asking for something in return. This triggered the principle of Reciprocity. As social beings, if we're given something, we typically have a strong urge to give back: we've been taught this since we were children. The need to return a favour is ingrained in all of us.

In this particular example, John got his appointment with the stakeholders in his target bank. By providing useful information, John made it easy for his contact to see the benefits of his product. Not only that, he also made it easy for his contact to create a case internally. John's contact didn't need to engage in effortful thinking about how this could work for him, or for the organisation.

On top of that, if others in his organisation agree it is an interesting prospect, he has a green light to organise meetings and demand people's time, without running the risk of looking foolish. Taking this approach meant that John had removed uncertainty, compelled his contact to reciprocate his efforts and made it easy to tell a good story internally.

Top things to take away

The point of this example is that an understanding of the principles of persuasion can help in any situation where influence is required. It doesn't matter if you are a start-up or working in a multi-national conglomerate – you are dealing with people, and the more you understand about the way people behave, the better placed you will be to get the outcomes you desire.

So, what can we learn from this story? Again, there are three key points here that you can start using to your advantage today.

1. **Find points of uncertainty and address them** – "System 1" thinking is intuitive, which is why it accounts for such a high percentage of our decision making. This intuition is what creates uncertainty when it comes to change, or promoting ideas. When you understand where your audience's uncertainty lies, you can address it to put them in a better position.

2. **Make it easy** – the easier something is to do, the more likely you are to do it. You know this yourself when it comes to booking things, taking exercise, changing habits. Make life easier for your audience, and your own job will become easier too.

3. **Help them out** – when you are seen to be giving something away or doing someone a favour, unconditionally, you activate the principle of Reciprocity and you are more likely to get something back in return. This often removes barriers that would be difficult to tackle otherwise.

Help people to say "yes"!

These examples demonstrate two things: the need to really consider the situation from the other person's point of view, and the need to look for the behavioural signals that point you to the areas you need to influence to help that person decide in your favour.

There's one big difference to consider, however. My banking case study is from 2008-2009, when everyone was in the office every day, there were fewer technological distractions, and it was easier to build good relationships.

Today, remote working, electronic communication and a lack of face-to-face familiarity make it arguably more difficult to build those crucial relationships and develop the trust you need. So you might have to work harder now than you may have done before. But the principles are still in play. They still work for me, and they will work for you too.

Further reading

Artinger, F.M., Artinger, S. and Gigerenzer, G. (2018) 'C. Y. A.: Frequency and causes of defensive decisions in Public Administration', Business Research, 12(1), pp. 9–25. doi:10.1007/s40685-018-0074-2.

Cialdini, R.B. (2021) Influence: The Psychology of Persuasion (new and expanded). New York: Harper Business.

Fogg, B.J. (2020) Tiny Habits: Why starting small makes lasting change easy. London: Virgin.

Gigerenzer, G. (2014). Risk savvy: How to make good decisions. New York, NY: Viking.

Kahneman, D. (2011) Thinking fast and slow. UK: Penguin Books.

And feel free to contact us at www.psybersafe.com/influence

Pilar Bringas
Cialdini Certified Coach in Ethical Persuasion

ABOUT THE AUTHOR: PILAR BRINGAS

Passionate about people and communications, curious from the cradle, endless learner and human optimist.

Pilar is a Cialdini Certified Coach and specialist in the art of influence and persuasion.

With ethics. With values. With scientific evidence.

Business advisor in marketing, communication and strategy
With more than 25 years of corporate experience in blue chip multinationals such as P&G, Heinz, LVMH, Apivita or ColArt, she has integrated 360° business vision, from production to customer service.

She has also been recognized and valued as a good leader of multicultural teams.

Last years, she has been working with small and medium companies in Spain, improving their market approach, leading their internationalization strategies and incorporating the digital tools into their processes.

Teacher and lecturer in marketing and communications
She works at the master & postgraduate programs of IESE Business School (regularly ranked amongst top 3 by Financial Times) and teaches in the Marketing Department of the Complutense University of Madrid.

Keynote Speaker
Pilar teaches, delivers talks, masterclasses and key notes in both Spanish and English.

Author of several books in Spanish "Marketing no es (solo) publicidad" (Marketing is not (just) advertising), "Influencia online" (Online Influence), this is her first collaboration in an English book

CHAPTER 7

The Macedonian maestro: Alexander the Great and the symphony of human behavior

History whispers tales of countless conquerors, but few resonate as powerfully as Alexander the Great. By his death at the tender age of 32, he had carved a path across continents, building an empire unparalleled in its time. Military prowess undoubtedly played a role, but delve deeper, and we discover a leader who mastered the art of understanding human behavior – a skill honed under the tutelage of the legendary philosopher, Aristotle.

A Young Prodigy and the Father of Persuasion

Alexander's brilliance wasn't solely forged in the fires of war. His education, nurtured by the legendary Aristotle, exposed him to a vast array of subjects. Aristotle, the "Father of Persuasion," instilled in Alexander the power of influencing behavior through reason and emotion. Imagine a young Alexander, under Aristotle's guidance, pondering the complexities of human psychology, the power of persuasion, and the importance of leadership that inspires, not just commands. These lessons became the foundation of Alexander's leadership style, transforming him from a prince into a maestro of human behavior.

Beyond the core principles of reason and emotion, Aristotle likely imparted two additional pillars of rhetoric that Alexander would masterfully wield:

- **The power of Logos: building arguments on logic and evidence**

Beyond understanding emotions and motivations, Aristotle championed the importance of **logos**, the appeal to reason and logic. Imagine young Alexander, under Aristotle's tutelage, meticulously dissecting historical battles, analysing strategies, and evaluating the role of logistics in achieving victory. Aristotle likely instilled in Alexander the importance of presenting clear arguments, backed by evidence and sound reasoning, to not only persuade his troops but also to secure alliances and garner support from conquered territories. This focus on logos would have equipped Alexander to be a more effective strategist and negotiator, able to sway others through logic and well-constructed arguments, not just brute force.

- **The art of Ethos: building credibility and trust**

Ethos, the appeal to the speaker's credibility and character, was another cornerstone of Aristotle's Rhetoric. Aristotle likely emphasized to Alexander the importance of leading by example, demonstrating courage, justice, and a sense of honour. Imagine young Alexander engaging in philosophical discussions with Aristotle, exploring the qualities of a virtuous leader. By embodying these values, Alexander could inspire loyalty and trust in his followers, fostering a sense of shared purpose that transcended simple military obligation. Moreover, by demonstrating respect for conquered cultures and adhering to a moral code, Alexander could project a strong ethos, earning the respect of not just his own troops but also the people he sought to integrate into his empire. This focus on ethos wouldn't just solidify Alexander's position as a powerful leader but also contribute to the long-term stability and cohesion of his empire.

Understanding needs and motivations: beyond brute force

Unlike many conquerors who relied solely on brute force, Alexander recognized the importance of understanding the needs and motivations of those he encountered. He incorporated conquered cultures into his empire, fostering a sense of unity and shared purpose. His ability to inspire loyalty and respect, not just fear, stemmed from this deep understanding of human behavior.

The case of Tyre: A Masterclass in Persuasion

Consider Alexander's siege of Tyre, a powerful Phoenician city-state. After months of relentless assault, the city remained defiant, perched on an island seemingly impregnable. Instead of resorting solely to brute force, Alexander, aware of the Tyrians' cultural and religious pride, devised a clever strategy. He ordered the construction of a massive mole, a land bridge connecting the island to the mainland. This not only provided a path for his soldiers but also threatened sacred temples on the outskirts of the city.

Alexander was always at the head of the battle, demonstrating his authority and leadership qualities. "The king himself climbed the highest siege-tower [which was full of catapults and other siege-engines]. His courage was great, but the danger greater for, conspicuous in his royal insignia and flashing armor, he was the prime target of enemy missiles. And his actions in the engagement were certainly spectacular."[1]

Leveraging his understanding of their cultural identity and emotional attachment to their city and religion, Alexander agreed to save those who had fled to the temples. He ensured his soldiers allowed the Tyrian population inside to remain, integrating them into his growing empire. By understanding the Tyrians' needs and motivations, he achieved victory through leadership and diplomacy, fostering a more cooperative relationship with the conquered city.

Beyond the battlefield, Alexander's story transcends military conquest. It's a testament to the power of understanding human behavior as a tool for building an empire. Building bridges across cultures, he fostered a fusion of Greek, Egyptian, and Persian traditions, laying the ground for a new Hellenistic era. He understood that a successful empire wasn't built solely on military might but on cultural understanding, respect for traditions, and the ability to inspire unity and shared purpose.

A legacy beyond conquest: the symphony of success in the modern world

Fast forward to today's fast-paced, technology-driven world, and the human melody remains the same.

Understanding and applying the science of human behavior, known as behavioral science, has become the key instrument for success.

The theories of several social scientific thinkers offer a clear picture: our decisions are far from perfectly logical, and emotions and biases play a significant role. Just to review some of them,

- **Herbert Simon** challenged the traditional economic model of "homo economicus" a perfectly rational actor who makes decisions based on complete information and perfect logic. For his work, he was awarded 1978 Nobel Memorial Prize in Economic Sciences.[2] His concept of **bounded rationality** acknowledges that humans have limited cognitive abilities and often rely on heuristics (mental shortcuts) to make decisions. This aligns with Alexander's understanding that his troops, while courageous, wouldn't be driven solely by logic on the battlefield. Leaders who recognize bounded rationality can create clear structures, provide relevant information, and anticipate potential biases to guide their teams towards optimal outcomes.

- **Daniel Kahneman's prospect theory** delves deeper into the emotional aspects of decision-making. His studies were also awarded by the Nobel Memorial Prize in Economic science in 2002.[3] It proposes that individuals exhibit loss aversion, feeling losses more acutely than gains. This can lead to risk-averse behavior when faced with potential losses. Imagine Alexander contemplating a daring maneuver. Prospect theory suggests he might be more likely to favor a safer strategy if framed in terms of potential losses (e.g., losing a significant number of soldiers). Leaders who understand prospect theory can frame decisions strategically, highlighting potential gains while acknowledging risks, fostering a more balanced approach.

- **Richard Thaler's endowment effect**, Nobel Prize winner in 2017,[4] explores how we value things we already own more than things we don't. This can manifest in situations like loyalty programs that reward continued patronage. Alexander likely recognized a similar phenomenon, offering conquered peoples a sense of ownership and a stake in the success of his empire, fostering a stronger sense of loyalty than mere subjugation. Leaders who understand the endowment effect can leverage it to create incentive structures that motivate desired behaviors.

- **Robert Cialdini** identified seven key principles of persuasion in his seminal work, **Influence, the psychology of persuasion.**[5] These principles – reciprocity, scarcity, authority, social proof, liking, commitment and consistency, and unity – resonate with Alexander's strategies. His willingness to engage in reciprocity with conquered peoples, the perceived scarcity of positions within his elite units, and the projection of authority through his lineage and victories all demonstrate an intuitive grasp of Cialdini's principles. Modern leaders who understand these principles can craft more persuasive communication strategies, fostering trust, collaboration, and ultimately, success.

By harnessing the insights of these behavioral scientists, we, like Alexander, can become conductors of human behavior, orchestrating success in a complex and ever-changing world.

Cognitive biases: the pitfalls of human decision-making

However, understanding the human mind extends beyond strengths to recognizing its limitations. Daniel Kahneman's prospect theory, a cornerstone of behavioral economics, sheds light on how our emotions and biases significantly influence our decision-making.

Imagine Alexander on the battlefield, facing a seemingly insurmountable enemy force. Kahneman's work suggests that Alexander, like any human leader, might be susceptible to overconfidence bias, potentially underestimating the enemy's strength. However, a leader who understands this bias can actively seek objective information and consult with advisors to mitigate its impact.

Beyond overconfidence, several other cognitive biases can cloud judgment:

- **Anchoring bias:** The tendency to rely too heavily on the first piece of information encountered when making a decision. Imagine Alexander, after a string of victories, being presented with an overly optimistic assessment of an opponent's weaknesses. Anchoring bias could lead him to underestimate the challenge and potentially overlook crucial preparations. A leader aware of this bias actively seeks diverse perspectives and avoids relying solely on initial impressions.

- **Confirmation bias:** The tendency to favour information that confirms existing beliefs and disregard contradictory evidence. Imagine Alexander surrounded by advisors who, basking in past victories, downplay the threat of a new enemy. Confirmation bias could lead him to overlook critical intelligence or dismiss warnings.

Leaders who mitigate this bias encourage healthy debate, actively seek out dissenting opinions, and ensure they have access to all available information.

- **Loss aversion:** The tendency to feel losses more acutely than gains. Imagine Alexander contemplating a risky battle strategy. Loss aversion could lead him to be overly cautious, potentially missing out on an opportunity for a decisive victory. Leaders aware of loss aversion can frame decisions around potential gains while acknowledging potential risks, striking a balance between calculated risks and measured action.

By understanding these plus the many other cognitive biases, leaders can make more informed decisions, navigate complex situations effectively, and ultimately achieve greater success.

Cialdini's seven principles: The symphony of influence

Robert Cialdini, another pivotal figure in behavioral science, identified the seven universal principles of influence: reciprocity, scarcity, authority, social proof, liking, commitment and consistency, and unity. Alexander, intuitively and unconsciously, understood these principles, applying them to remarkable effect.

- **Reciprocity**: When ambassadors from conquered cities brought gifts, Alexander often responded with even more generous offerings, not just building a sense of obligation but also fostering their loyalty.

- **Social Proof**: The resounding of his victories and the generous conditions of surrender for his enemies preceded his conquests. After the Tyre events and because they wanted to get rid of their Persian masters, the complete Egypt Empire surrendered to Alexander and he was crowned pharaoh without shedding a drop of blood.[6]

- **Unity**: Public displays of recognition for successful soldiers and the incorporation of conquered peoples into his elite units rein-forced a sense of belonging and the desire to be part of the winning team.

These principles remain relevant today. Businesses utilize **reciprocity** by offering loyalty programs and gifts. Social media platforms thrive on the power of **social proof**, displaying likes and shares to influence user behavior. Moreover, they are constantly looking to increase their user's engagement to build into the **unity** principle.

A bridge to modern Leadership

Consider the ever-evolving business landscape. We've moved from the volatile, uncertain, complex, and ambiguous (VUCA) world to the even more challenging BANI environment – brittle, anxious, non-linear, and incomprehensible.[7] Leaders who can navigate this complexity must be attuned to the anxieties and decision-making processes of their teams.

Alexander's success wasn't solely his own doing. He surrounded him-self with talented advisors, generals, and soldiers, understanding the importance of teamwork and building a strong supporting cast. His abil-ity to delegate tasks, empower individuals, and leverage their unique strengths mirrors the importance of fostering effective team dynamics in modern organizations.

Let's explore how Alexander's legacy translates into practical strategies for navigating the complexities of the modern world:

- **Understanding needs and motivations:** Studies reveal that CEOs spend a staggering 85% of their time communicating – speeches, meetings, and connecting with teams. Effective lead-ers strive to understand the needs and motivations of those they lead, whether employees, customers, or partners. A company that understands its employees' needs for career growth and development can create a more engaged and productive work-force. Similarly, a marketing team that identifies a customer's desire for convenience and affordability can develop targeted campaigns that resonate deeply.

- **The power of persuasion:** Effective communication is not just for the C-suite; it's the lifeblood of any organization. Leaders who excel at active listening, tailoring messages to their audience, and clear expression become better persuaders, fostering a sense of shared vision and purpose. Alexander's ability to rally his troops through powerful speeches and strategic decisions is mirrored in modern leaders who utilize clear communication, storytelling, and emotional appeals to motivate their teams. Effective communication builds trust and inspires action.

- **Building bridges across cultures:** In today's globalized world, fostering understanding and respect across diverse cultures is essential for success. Alexander's integration of conquered cultures laid the groundwork for a more interconnected world. Modern businesses operating internationally must be culturally sensitive, adapting their strategies and communication styles to resonate with different audiences. By doing so, they foster trust and strengthen partnerships, paving the way for success in the global marketplace.

- **Leadership and social influence:** Effective leaders today must understand how to influence and inspire others. The World Economic Forum in its "Future of Jobs" report emphasizes the critical importance of leadership and social influence in the future of work. The ability to persuade and influence others is a core and highly sought-after skill across diverse industries.

The Symphony continues: a legacy of understanding

Alexander the Great's legacy transcends military conquests. It's a testament to the power of understanding human behavior as a tool for success. He wasn't just a conqueror; he was a leader who built an empire on the foundation of cultural understanding, persuasion, and inspiring a shared vision. By harnessing the power of behavioral science, we become conductors of human behavior, orchestrating success in a complex and ever-changing world.

Managers get the work done through people. They allocate the resources, direct the activities of others, and take decisions to attain organizational goals. Every organization is a coordinated social unit, composed of two or more people, which functions to achieve a common goal. The leadership team is responsible for the functioning of the organization. As the world has become a global village, understanding human behavior has become a critical skill for managers today as it helps management to:

- become flexible and proactive, enabling it to lead the organization on a global scale.

- effectively deal with work force diversity by promoting its awareness, increasing diversity skills and encouraging culture and gender diversity.

- develop resilience, human strength, and foster vitality empowering their employees, as they are the major forces for implementing any change.

Balancing behavioral science with responsibility

While understanding human behavior grants immense power, wielding that power ethically is paramount. The lessons gleaned from Alexander the Great, and the insights of behavioral science can be immensely valuable, but only if applied with a commitment to ethical persuasion, not manipulative exploitation. Let's delve deeper into the ethical considerations of applying behavioral science in the modern business world.

Persuasion vs. Manipulation

The line between persuasion and manipulation can be deceptively thin. **Persuasion** aims to influence decisions through reason, logic, and emotional appeals that resonate with the audience's needs. It empowers individuals to make informed choices that align with their best interests.

Manipulation, however, seeks to control behavior through deceptive tactics, exploiting vulnerabilities, and disregarding the well-being of the target. Think of manipulative marketing tactics that prey on insecurities or create a false sense of urgency to push unnecessary purchases. This approach erodes trust and breeds resentment, ultimately harming a company's reputation and long-term success.

So, how can we navigate the ethical terrain of behavioral science applications? Here are some crucial areas to consider:

- **Transparency and disclosure:** Be upfront about your intentions. Explain how data is collected and used. Transparency fosters trust and ensures informed decision-making. For instance, a company offering loyalty rewards should clearly outline the program's terms and conditions, avoiding hidden fees or surprise expiration dates.

- **Respect for autonomy:** Recognize that individuals have the right to make their own choices. Nudges and incentives can be helpful but avoid creating a coercive environment. For example, a fitness app could offer badges and challenges to motivate users, but refrain from bombarding them with guilt-inducing messages if they miss a workout session.

- **Focus on long-term benefits:** Ethical persuasion aims for mutually beneficial outcomes. A pricing strategy utilizing scarcity tactics might temporarily boost sales, but if the product itself is poor quality, it leads to customer dissatisfaction and lost trust in the long run. Building customer loyalty through ethical persuasion

– offering a quality product at a fair price, providing exceptional customer service – ensures sustainable success.

- **Avoid exploitation of biases:** While understanding biases is valuable, don't exploit them to manipulate vulnerable individuals. For instance, a website applying the endowment effect shouldn't create a false sense of scarcity to induce panic purchases.

The ethical imperative in business: why it matters

"Rhetoric is the faculty of finding the available means of persuasion [...] and it is useful because what it is true and just naturally prevails over opposites."

(Aristotle, Rhetoric 2nd book).

In the competitive business landscape, prioritizing ethical persuasion offers several compelling advantages:

- **Building trust and loyalty:** Customers who feel respected and valued are more likely to become loyal patrons. Ethical marketing fosters brand affinity, encouraging word-of-mouth recommendations and repeat business.

- **Enhanced employee engagement:** Employees who feel their well-being is considered are more productive and engaged. Leaders who understand behavioral science can create a workplace environment that motivates and rewards positive contributions.

- **Sustainable growth:** Ethical practices foster a positive company reputation, attracting and retaining top talent, investors, and customer loyalty, leading to sustainable long-term growth.

- **Mitigating risks:** Manipulative tactics can backfire, leading to legal repercussions, brand damage, and consumer backlash. Ethical practices minimize such risks, contributing to business stability and resilience.

On the other hand, according to the studies of Dr. Robert Cialdini, the systematic use of unethical practices will lead to financial malfunctioning due to hidden costs and employee malfeasance.

He calls them the three tumors. Unethical practices eventually will provoke a rotten mechanism:

- Poor employee performance due to "ethical stress" caused by having to do things against their own values.

- High employee turnover, as those whose values conflict with the job will search for new jobs and leave as soon as they can.

- Employee fraud because the remaining employees will be those comfortable with cheating.

Cialdini affirms that when the principles are honestly and genuinely present in a given situation, it is recommendable to use them.

"Ethically used, the principles will always guide us through the right path, we benefit the world and we all win."

Just as Aristotle stated 4th century BCE. And surely, this was a piece of advice Alexander the Great took from him, as we all should. Most of us will not conquer foreign lands but we can conquer minds, ethically.

The final note: a conductor of human potential

Just as Alexander, under Aristotle's tutelage, learned to understand the intricacies of human psychology, so too can we equip ourselves with the tools of behavioral science.

By adopting an ethical approach to behavioral science, businesses can become true conductors of human behavior, orchestrating success in a socially responsible manner. Just as Alexander the Great's legacy transcends military conquests, our goal should not just be to influence behavior, but to do so with integrity and respect for human autonomy.

By studying persuasion techniques, understanding human biases, and prioritizing clear communication, we can become leaders worthy of the title, leading our teams and organizations to a resounding crescendo of success. And by prioritizing ethical persuasion, we can create a symphony of success that benefits both businesses and individuals, leading to a more prosperous and equitable world.

The world may no longer be dominated by empires, but the symphony of human behavior continues to play, and those who understand its melodies are the ones who will truly thrive.

REFERENCES

1. Quintus Curtius Rufus " History of Alexander the Great of Macedonia ", the fall of Tyre, section 4.4.10-21

2. https://www.kva.se/en/prizes/prize-in-economic-sciences/laureates/?

3. https://www.kva.se/en/prizes/prize-in-economic-sciences/laureates/?

4. https://www.kva.se/en/prizes/prize-in-economic-sciences/laureates/?

5. Cialdini, R.B. (1984), " INFLUENCE. The psychology of persuasion ". Ed. Harper Collins, expanded edition 2021

6. https://www.ucl.ac.uk/museums-static/digitalegypt/chronology/alexandergreat.html

7. https://hagergroup.com/en/blog/trends-innovation/vuca-bani

Isto Felin

Cialdini Certified Coach in Ethical Persuasion, Strategic Renewal Consultant

ABOUT THE AUTHOR: ISTO FELIN

It's the human element that needs more attention than ever in today's businesses.

When business leaders strive for growth and strategic renewal through the means of their people, Isto Felin is the injection of innovation and transformative power to make it happen.

Isto's unique blend of academic inquisition, practical experience, and innovative thinking make him a sought-after international consultant, coach, and speaker in the business world.

In 2023, as the renowned behavioural scientist *Dr. Robert Cialdini* set up the Cialdini Institute for Ethical Influence, Isto became a **Cialdini Certified Coach**, solidifying his position as a leading expert in ethical influence.

With a background in top-tier management consulting at firms like Deloitte, Isto honed his expertise in growth strategies, innovation, and performance improvement. Today, he serves as a Strategic Renewal Consultant for Hanken & SSE Executive Education (https://www.hankensse.fi/), where he helps organisations navigate complex change and drive sustainable growth.

Combining his Master's degree in Business Administration and Design Business Management with his consulting experience, Isto has founded **Growth Discovery** (https://www.growthdiscovery.io/). This venture leverages scientifically-backed methods for growth, focusing on **Tiny Influence Tweaks for Mighty Business Results** or **TIMBR.** By going to **https://www.growthdiscovery.io/TIMBR/,** you can claim your "TIMBR" book bonus.

Isto's work currently spans the Western world, reaching from North America to the UK, and Northern Europe. His mission is to *"Happily Influence People,"* whether working with management teams seeking strategic direction, sales organisations aiming to boost commercial results, or customer engagement operations striving for exceptional experiences. In each case, it is the human side of change that directs his work.

As a Finnish citizen, Isto is keenly connected to his roots. He enjoys sauna relaxation and gaining energy from the beautiful Finnish forests and lakes. Isto appreciates modern art, design and architecture, but most of all, he loves and is supported by his family of six.

You can connect with Isto on LinkedIn at **https://www.linkedin.com/in/ifelin/.** Just drop a note that you read this book and you'll be sent a nice surprise.

CHAPTER 8

The TIMBR Effect: Tiny Tweaks, Mighty Results in Business

Have you ever wondered how a single sentence can change everything? Imagine you're watching a favourite TV singing contest. The lights dim, and a contestant walks on stage. You can't see them yet, but you hear the first notes of a country song:

Baby, lock the door and turn the lights down low...

The voice is deep, warm and charismatic. Two judges, a famous rapper and a pop star, spin their chairs around, eager to coach this mystery singer. As the lights come up, you see a cowboy hat and boots. The audience cheers, and there's an instant connection between the singer and the pop star.

The pop star makes his pitch: "I love country music! I'd follow Brad Paisley around the world. We're a perfect match!"

It seems like a done deal. But then, the rapper says something unexpected: "Will it be Paisley, or will you want to take a risk? You know that the latest musical successes come from collaborations between country and rap."

The cowboy hesitates. "You're right! Why did you have to say that?"

Then another pause. "The excitement of a child in me perhaps wants to do something crazy, so I'll go with you."

In a surprising twist, the cowboy chooses the rapper as his coach. One short sentence changed everything.

This is the power of influence. It's not about manipulation or trickery. It's about understanding how people think and make decisions. In business, mastering ethical influence can be the difference between success and stagnation.

As a management consultant, I've spent years honing these skills. I've discovered that tiny influence tweaks can lead to mighty business results – what I call **TIMBR**. Let me take you on a journey through the world of ethical persuasion in business, and show you how TIMBR can transform your approach to growth and success, and surely hearing YES more often.

The Invisible Force: Influence in Motion

Think back to the last time you made a big decision. Maybe you were choosing a new phone, recruiting a new team member, or picking an advisor for your business. You probably thought you were being completely logical, weighing pros and cons carefully. But what if I told you that invisible forces were guiding your choice?

These invisible forces are the principles of persuasion, identified by Dr. Robert Cialdini through years of scientific research. They're like the secret ingredients in a master chef's recipe – subtle, but powerful. When used ethically in business, they can create remarkable results.

There are sometimes concerns that, in a B2B setting, the principles do not apply or have the full effect, although they are commonly used in sales, sometimes unknowingly. Some may argue that in a business setting, we only make rational decisions. We may believe that decisions are solely based on facts and only as all aspects of data are reviewed and performance is measured.

Dr. Cialdini's research has shown time and time again, that this is not true. As you can apply the principles of persuasion in a business setting you can expect a major increase in your results. It is because the B2B setting is no different from a B2C or an interpersonal setting in terms of who is involved. In each case, we are dealing with humans. And human-to-human interaction is the core of any type of business activity.

In an age where different types of literacy can be reproduced and sometimes even replaced with technology, the need for human competencies is vital. The skill of ethically influencing people, especially in a business setting, is crucial for economic sustainability and value creation. Those people and organisations that constantly learn and ethically influence others in their daily work and communication will be the ones to stand out in the future and create a growth path for themselves and those they collaborate with. The World Economic Forum and Forbes have listed influence as a top in-demand power skill in today's business environment.

The TIMBR Effect: Felling Giants with Precision

Imagine standing at the edge of a vast forest. Towering before you is an enormous redwood—a titan of the woods, stretching hundreds of feet into the sky. Your task? To bring it down. You lack huge machinery, but in your hands, you hold a professional-grade chainsaw—powerful, yet requiring skill and precision to use effectively.

This scenario mirrors the challenges we often face in business. Those enormous redwoods? They're the seemingly insurmountable obstacles – we call them influence challenges: resistant clients, entrenched competitors, or rigid organisational structures. And that chainsaw? It's **TIMBR—Tiny Influence for Mighty Business Results**. With a tiny effort using influence, sometimes only replacing one word, you can get huge gains. The return on investment will surprise you. These tiny tweaks lead you to hear the right kind of YES you want more often.

In the world of logging, experienced woodsmen know that felling a giant tree isn't about brute force. It's about precision, patience, and understanding the tree's structure. Let's break down the process:

1. Observation

Before firing up the chainsaw, a skilled logger studies the tree. They consider its lean, the direction of the wind, and the safest path for it to fall. In business, this is our research phase. We analyze the situation, understand the key players, and identify potential obstacles and opportunities. We might also frame the situation with pre-suasive tactics, focusing the attention of your counterpart in a mutually favorable direction.

2. The Face Cut

The logger begins with a precise, angled cut on the side of the tree facing the intended fall direction. This seemingly small notch will ultimately guide the entire tree's descent. In TIMBR terms, this is our initial approach—the carefully chosen influence principle that sets the stage for everything that follows.

3. The Back Cut

On the opposite side, the logger makes a horizontal cut, slightly higher than the base of the face cut. As this cut progresses, the tree begins to lean, guided by the face cut. In business, this represents our consistent application of influence techniques, steadily moving our "target" in the desired direction and combining other persuasion principles with the initial one.

4. The Hinge

A thin strip of wood left between the face cut and back cut acts as a hinge, controlling the tree's fall. In TIMBR, this is the delicate balance we maintain, ensuring our influence remains ethical and aligned with both our goals and our client's best interests.

5. The Felling Wedges

Loggers often use plastic or metal wedges to help direct the fall or prevent the chainsaw from getting pinched. These small tools can make a massive difference in the outcome. Similarly, in TIMBR, small "wedges" of additional influence principles can tip the scales in crucial moments.

6. The Moment of Truth

When all cuts are made correctly, the mighty tree begins to fall, often with a series of loud cracks as wood fibers snap. In business, this is when we see our influence pay off—when a client makes a decision, a team aligns with a new strategy, or a market shifts in our favor.

7. Clean-up and Processing

After the tree falls, loggers use their chainsaws to remove branches and cut the trunk into manageable sections. In TIMBR, this is our follow-through—ensuring that the changes we've influenced are implemented effectively and yield the expected results for the long term.

Just as a skilled logger can bring down a massive tree with a series of precise cuts from their chainsaw, TIMBR allows us to tackle enormous business challenges through small, strategic applications of influence.

Remember, the goal isn't to manipulate or force outcomes. Like sustainable logging practices that maintain forest health, ethical influence should create value for all parties involved. It's about guiding decisions and behaviors in a way that benefits everyone—just as a well-felled tree provides valuable timber without damaging the surrounding forest.

So the next time you're faced with a towering business or influence challenge, don't be intimidated by its size. Remember the logger with their chainsaw. With TIMBR, you have the tools to fell giants, one precise cut at a time. It's not about having the biggest saw; it's about the sharpness of your saw and knowing exactly where and how to apply your influence for maximum impact.

In the forest of business, be the skilled woodsman, not the bulldozer. With TIMBR, you'll find that even the mightiest redwoods can be brought down with precision, patience, and the right application of your influence chainsaw.

Let's explore how these principles work in the real world of business, using my own experiences as a guide.

The Software Revolution: A Case Study in Persuasion

Picture this: It's 2015, and I'm working with a large financial services company. We've discovered an exciting new technology called Robotic Process Automation (RPA). Imagine software that can mimic human actions on a computer – clicking, typing, copying, and pasting – but faster and without errors. It's like having a tireless digital worker who never needs a coffee break.

The potential was huge. This technology could streamline operations, reduce errors, and free up employees for more creative and valuable work. But there was a problem: hardly anyone was using it at the time. How could we convince our client to take a chance on this unfamiliar technology?

This is where the principles of ethical persuasion came into play. Let me break down how we used them:

1. **Reciprocity**: We freely shared our knowledge and experience about RPA, even before the client committed to working with us. When you give something valuable, people naturally want to give back.

2. **Unity**: We positioned ourselves as partners in their digital transformation journey, not just outside consultants. People are more influenced by others they perceive as part of their group.

3. **Liking**: We built genuine relationships with our clients, finding common ground and shared interests. We even admitted we didn't know everything about the technology, but were skilled in finding out. People prefer to say yes to those they know and like.

4. **Social Proof**: We showed our client that other respected organisations, like the NHS (National Health Service) in the United Kingdom, were already using RPA successfully. People tend to follow the lead of similar others, especially in unfamiliar situations.

5. **Authority**: We referred to experts and cited, for example, Gartner and other reputable sources to back up our claims. People are more likely to follow the lead of credible, knowledgeable authorities.

6. **Commitment and Consistency**: We reminded our client of their recent commitment to quality improvement (they had just achieved ISO 9001 certification). People strive to be consistent with their past actions and statements.

7. **Scarcity**: We emphasized that early adopters of this technology would have a significant advantage over competitors. The fear of missing out is a powerful motivator.

The result? Our client decided to pilot the RPA technology. Within days, they saw improvements in efficiency and accuracy in chosen business processes. This early adoption gave them a significant advantage as the technology became more widespread.

But here's the real magic: we didn't just use these principles randomly. We carefully considered which ones would be most effective based on our client's goals and motivations. Let's look at how this worked.

The Hidden Framework: Aligning Persuasion with Motivation

Imagine you're trying to build a house. You wouldn't just start nailing boards together randomly, right? You'd need a blueprint – a plan that shows how all the pieces fit together.

Choosing your focus of influence is like a blueprint for persuasion. It helps us understand why certain principles work better in different situations. Here's a simple breakdown:

- If you want to **build trust with your client**, focus on reciprocity, liking and unity.

- If you want to **help your client feel secure**, emphasize social proof and authority.

- If you want to **help your client commit**, lean on commitment & consistency, and scarcity.

In our RPA case, we were dealing with all three areas of focus to get the best outcome:

1. We needed to build and earn our client's trust to build a lasting relationship.

2. We had to help our client feel secure about a new technology.

3. We wanted to help our client commit to a pilot case and implement RPA.

By understanding how each principle is connected to a certain focus, we could choose the most effective persuasion principles for each aspect of our pitch. This is the strategic approach that TIMBR represents – Tiny Influence for Mighty Business Results.

TIMBR in Action: Small Changes, Big Impact

Ok, you might be thinking, "this all sounds great, but does it really make a difference in the real business world?" Let me share a few more examples of how TIMBR has created remarkable results for businesses across various industries.

Case Study 1: The Reluctant Retailer

A large retail chain was hesitant to invest in a new nationwide customer experience program. They worried about the costs and complexity of implementation. Here's how we used TIMBR:

1. **Social Proof:** We showed case studies of similar retailers who had successfully implemented training programs.

2. **Liking:** We introduced a co-creation and cooperation model where we trained each store manager to then train the staff. This brought costs down and created commitment.

3. **Reciprocity:** We offered freely of our experience of what has worked elsewhere to significantly improve customer service, experience and sales results.

Result: The retailer agreed to the initial one-off program, which was so successful that they continued the program five years in a row. As a result, being the incumbent in the market, they saw the highest growth each year of all the players as this training program was in place.

Case Study 2: The Painful Transformation

A mid-sized technology company had devised a turnaround growth strategy, but could not engage long-timers in the change process. We applied TIMBR like this:

1. **Authority:** We gained approval from the company president for the program and built extra value and prestige for the participants.

2. **Commitment and Consistency:** We reminded the transformation program participants of their stated company values, which included constant renewal and succeeding together.

3. **Unity:** We positioned the transformative strategy as a team effort, involving the old-timers in designing how the strategy should be executed in their units.

Result: The company moved forward with the transformation, and the old-timers were key in achieving much-needed business renewal for growth. The company was a stock market star for several years as a result.

In these cases, we didn't rely on a single persuasion principle. We carefully and thoughtfully combined multiple principles, aligned them with the needed focus, and applied them with precision. That's the essence of TIMBR – small, strategic changes that yield outsized results.

The Ethical Edge: Why TIMBR Matters

Now, you might be wondering: "Isn't all this persuasion just manipulation? Is it really ethical?"

This is a crucial question, and it's at the heart of why TIMBR is so powerful. Ethical influence isn't about tricking people or pressuring them into decisions they'll regret. It's about presenting information and opportunities in a way that resonates with how our brains intuitively make decisions.

When used ethically, TIMBR creates win-win situations. It helps businesses communicate their value more effectively, and it helps customers and clients make decisions that truly benefit them. It's about aligning interests, not exploiting weaknesses.

Consider our RPA case study. By implementing this technology, our client was able to:

- Free up employees from repetitive tasks, allowing them to focus on more rewarding work
- Improve efficiency and reduce errors, leading to better service for their customers
- Be consistent with their commitment to constant development and quality
- Gain a competitive edge in their industry

You will find a table at the end of this chapter (bonus section) that shows you how the TIMBR effect was used in the RPA case and my consulting work, and how you might apply each principle in your business context.

These are real, tangible benefits. Our use of persuasion principles didn't create these benefits – it simply helped our client overcome their initial hesitation and see the true value of the opportunity.

This is why mastering ethical influence is so crucial in today's business world. In an age of information overload and constant distraction, the ability to communicate effectively and persuade ethically is more valuable than ever.

Your TIMBR Journey: Next Steps

By now, you're probably curious about how you can apply TIMBR in your own business or career. Here are three paths you can take:

1. Do-It-Yourself Approach

Start by observing influence principles in action around you. Notice how advertisers, politicians, and even your friends use these techniques. Then, experiment with applying them in your own communications and always consider the ethics. By being an exceptional noticer, you will become better with each new influence challenge. For support, go to **https://www.growthdiscovery.io/TIMBR/**.

2. Be trained by Dr Robert Cialdini himself

I offer a comprehensive online course on Ethical Influence by Dr Robert Cialdini where he walks you through each persuasion principle and how to apply it ethically in business and personal settings. You'll get case studies, practical exercises, and personalized feedback. And, of course, you get certified as an Ethical Influence Practitioner. Learn more about the course at **https://bit.ly/cialdini-certification/**. If you are concerned about making an investment (with a great return), please contact me to make sure you get your investment's worth.

3. Get professionally supported on your TIMBR journey

I offer coaching and team training sessions to complement Dr Cialdini's online course (path #2). This will accelerate your learning and take it to a more actionable level for results. It's not the learning that will be valuable to you, but the application of it. We'll work together to identify your specific influence challenges and develop tailored TIMBR strategies. Once again, the only thing to do is go to **https://www.growthdiscovery.io/TIMBR/**.

Whichever path you choose, remember this: mastering ethical influence is a journey, not a solution or destination. It's a skill that you'll continue to refine and improve. I'm also constantly learning new things about how people behave and make decisions.

The Choice Is Yours

Remember our singing cowboy? He faced a choice between the familiar path (choosing the country music-loving pop star) and the risky but potentially rewarding path (choosing the rapper). With a single sentence, the rapper got a YES from the cowboy. What principles of persuasion were in use here? And why was the rapper chosen over the pop star – didn't the pop star use unity to connect with the cowboy? Here is a breakdown of the principles used:

Principles that were used to influence the contestant in making a selection

Persuasion principle used	A DECENT PITCH: Pop Star Judge: "I love country music! I'd follow Brad Paisley around the world. We're a perfect match!"	A MUCH BETTER PITCH TO HEAR A 'YES': Rapper Judge: "Will it be Paisley, or will you want to take a risk? You know that the latest musical successes have come from collaborations between country and rap."
Unity	Found a commonality in country music and made that known to the contestant.	Although the rapper leaned on the cowboy's musical genre, what united the two more was the "excitement to do something crazy" giving a sense of co-creation as two different genres unite.
Commitment and Consistency	Offered the safe option consistent with the contestant's musical genre.	The rapper didn't know it at first, but the suggestion of taking a risk and being adventurous triggered a feeling of commitment and consistency as the pitch brought childhood memories and excitement to the surface which screamed for action.
Scarcity	Did not exhibit this an option that was scarce..	By mentioning a collaboration option outside the cowboy contestant's genre, the rapper offered an opportunity the contestant stood to lose. This was a one-time chance.

G GROWTH DISCOVERY

Happily Influencing People

For more learning on TIMBR go to:

https://www.growthdiscovery.io/TIMBR/

In business, we face similar choices every day. Do we stick with what's comfortable, or do we take calculated risks that could lead to breakthrough success? The power of persuasion principles is in combining them, as well as activating and amplifying them at the right time. Still, it is not advisable to pile up as many persuasion tactics as possible, because in some cases they can have the opposite effect when those being persuaded feel they are being manipulated. Once again, it is important to keep ethics in mind and ensure that we are always smart, truthful and understanding of each context so it is indeed beneficial to our counterpart.

There is no book shelf solution. Although we can identify patterns in using these principles, each influence challenge requires a tailored process to seek out the right combination of actions.

TIMBR gives you the tools to make those choices with confidence. It helps you communicate more effectively, build stronger relationships, and create more value for your customers and clients.

So, what will your choice be? Will you stick with the familiar, or will you take a risk and explore the power of ethical influence?

If you're ready to start your TIMBR journey, I invite you to reach out. Visit **www.growthdiscovery.io/TIMBR/** to receive exclusive insight from me as a bonus for picking up this book.

Good job! The insight shows you more ways to activate and amplify the power of persuasion in your business. You also have a chance to explore how we can work together to unlock your influence potential and drive remarkable business growth.

After all, in the world of business, as in music, sometimes the most beautiful harmonies come from unexpected collaborations. Are you ready to compose your success story?

Your bonus section: TIMBR in Practice

To help you start applying TIMBR in your business context, here's a table summarizing the seven principles of persuasion, how I have used them in my advisory services, and how you might apply them in your business:

My focus	Persuasion principle used	How I applied the TIMBR effect with my clients	How you can use the TIMBR effect in your business
Building trust with client	Reciprocity	I listen carefully and offer valuable insights and resources upfront, before any formal engagement.	You can provide free trials, samples, or expert advice. Don't position yourself to respond or get some result, seek to listen and give of yourself.
Building trust with client	Unity	I seek for co-creation opportunities and position myself as a partner in my clients' growth journey, not just an outside consultant.	You can create a strong brand community, emphasising shared values and goals with your customers. Take time to get to know your client also at a personal level.
Building trust with client	Liking	I take time to build genuine relationships with clients, finding common ground beyond just business.	You can train your team in relationship-building skills and encourage them to find authentic connections with customers. Clients like you when you like them first.
Helping client feel secure	Social Proof	I share case studies and testimonials from similar businesses that have succeeded with our strategies.	You can showcase customer reviews, user statistics, or industry awards on your website and marketing materials.
Helping client feel secure	Authority	I leverage my partnerships with respected figures like Dr. Cialdini and share my expertise through publications and speaking engagements.	You can highlight your team's credentials, industry certifications, or media appearances.
Helping client commit	Commitment and Consistency	I remind clients of their stated goals and values, aligning our work with their existing commitments.	You can highlight customers' past choices and how your new offering aligns with those decisions.
Helping client commit	Scarcity	When my offering is limited, I make that known to my client and emphasise the opportunity cost of delaying.	Use truthful limited-time promotions, exclusive offers, or emphasize unique features that competitors don't have.

GROWTH DISCOVERY

For more learning on TIMBR go to:

https://www.growthdiscovery.io/TIMBR/

Happily Influencing People

Remember, the key to TIMBR is not just using these principles, but using them strategically and ethically. Always consider your audience and what needs to be developed (building trust or helping the client to feel secure or commit) and choose the principles that best align with those motives.

With practice and persistence, you'll soon see how these tiny influence tweaks can indeed lead to mighty business results. For more learning on applying these principles and TIMBR, go to **https://www.growthdiscovery.io/TIMBR/**

Epilogue

Thank you for investing in this book. We hope you enjoyed it and that it will yield a great return in years to come. If you think this book might be useful to others, please share it with them.

We know that knowledge alone does not lead to effective application. The key to mastering the principles of persuasion is to put them into practice. The best way to do this is to start recognising which principles to use in a given situation and how.

Going over the practical application of influence and persuasion with a certified coach will fast-track your understanding and application skills. That will enable you to recognise the opportunities around you on a daily basis and avoid missing out on the levers available to you.

Here are some final words of encouragement from each of the authors:

Patrick: When facing an influence challenge, take some time to calmly review the list of principles and see which ones you can uncover. Remember that Contrast is always there.

Leopold: You can't influence people unless you first give them a piece of you. Reflect, Identify it, and distil it into a Powerline — then watch your worth amplified.

John: The difference between the amateur and the professional speaker is an understanding of how our minds work – the 7 principles of influence in this book are the key to all great communication.

James: Words have power, so remember to slow down and, where possible, consciously choose the most persuasive words for the situation.

Martin: Knowing the principles of persuasion and how to use them will bring you transformational results. As fellow humans, even your toughest stakeholders can be won over to your way of thinking.

Mark: It doesn't matter whether you are a start-up or working in a multinational conglomerate – you are dealing with people, and the more you understand the way people behave, the better placed you will be to get the outcomes you desire.

Pilar: Empires may no longer dominate the world, but the symphony of human behavior continues to play, and those who understand its melodies are the ones who will truly thrive.

Isto: Make a habit of using at least one principle in your daily interactions, and before you know it, you will become skillful in creating a mighty impact on others with tiny means.

When you're ready to take the next step, feel free to reach out to any of us authors. We'll be happy to talk with you and work out the best next steps for you.

We wish you an inspired journey to hearing more YES in your life.

www.ingramcontent.com/pod-product-compliance
Lightning Source LLC
Chambersburg PA
CBHW070923270326
41927CB00011B/2694